The Eighty Years' War

The Eighty Years' War

The War between the Dutch and the Spanish in
the Netherlands, 1568–1648

Thomas Grattan

LEONAUR

The Eighty Years' War
The War between the Dutch and the Spanish in the Netherlands, 1568-1648
by Thomas Grattan

FIRST EDITION

Leonaur is an imprint of Oakpast Ltd

Copyright in this form © 2019 Oakpast Ltd

ISBN: 978-1-78282-820-4 (hardcover)
ISBN: 978-1-78282-821-1 (softcover)

http://www.leonaur.com

Publisher's Notes

Contents

Chapter 1

1555–1566

The Netherlands were never in a more flourishing state than at the accession of Philip II. The external relations of the country presented an aspect of prosperity and peace. England was closely allied to it by Queen Mary's marriage with Philip; France, fatigued with war, had just concluded with it a five years' truce; Germany, paralyzed by religious dissensions, exhausted itself in domestic quarrels; the other states were too distant or too weak to inspire any uneasiness; and nothing appeared wanting for the public weal. Nevertheless, there was something dangerous and alarming in the situation of the Low Countries; but the danger consisted wholly in the connexion between the monarch and the people, and the alarm was not sounded till the mischief was beyond remedy.

From the time that Charles V. was called to reign over Spain, he may be said to have been virtually lost to the country of his birth. He was no longer a mere Duke of Brabant or Limberg, a Count of Flanders or Holland; he was also King of Castile, Aragon, Leon, and Navarre, of Naples, and of Sicily. These various kingdoms had interests evidently opposed to those of the Low Countries, and forms of government far different. It was scarcely to be doubted that the absolute monarch of so many people would look with a jealous eye on the institutions of those provinces which placed limits to his power; and the natural consequence was, that he who was a legitimate king in the south soon degenerated into a usurping master in the north.

But during the reign of Charles the danger was in some measure lessened, or at least concealed from public view, by the apparent facility with which he submitted to and observed the laws and customs of his native country. With Philip, the case was far different, and the results too obvious. Uninformed on the Belgian character, despising the state of manners, and ignorant of the language, no sympathy attached him to the people. He brought with him to the throne all the hostile prejudices of a foreigner, without one of the kindly or considerate feelings of a compatriot.

Spain, where this young prince had hitherto passed his life, was in some degree excluded from European civilization. A contest of seven centuries between the Mahomedan tribes and the descendants of the Visigoths, cruel, like all civil wars, and, like all those of religion, not merely a contest of rulers, but essentially of the people, had given to the manners and feelings of this unhappy country a deep stamp of barbarity. The ferocity of military chieftains had become the basis of the government and laws. The Christian kings had adopted the perfidious and bloody system of the despotic *sultans* they replaced. Magnificence and tyranny, power and cruelty, wisdom and dissimulation, respect and fear, were inseparably associated in the minds of a people so governed. They comprehended nothing in religion but a God armed with omnipotence and vengeance, or in politics but a king as terrible as the deity he represented.

Philip, bred in this school of slavish superstition, taught that he was the despot for whom it was formed, familiar with the degrading tactics of eastern tyranny, was at once the most contemptible and unfortunate of men. Isolated from his kind, and wishing to appear superior to those beyond whom his station had placed him, he was insensible to the affections which soften and ennoble human nature. He was perpetually filled with one idea—that of his greatness; he had but one ambition—that of command; but one enjoyment—that of exciting fear. Victim to this revolting selfishness, his heart was never free from care; and the bitter melancholy of his character seemed to nourish a desire of evil-doing, which irritated suffering often produces in man. Deceit and blood were his greatest, if not his only, delights. The religious zeal which he affected, or felt, showed itself but in acts of cruelty; and the fanatic bigotry which inspired him formed the strongest contrast to the divine spirit of Christianity.

Nature had endowed this ferocious being with wonderful penetration and unusual self-command; the first revealing to him the views of others, and the latter giving him the surest means of counteracting them, by enabling him to control himself. Although ignorant, he had a prodigious instinct of cunning. He wanted courage, but its place was supplied by the harsh obstinacy of wounded pride. All the corruptions of intrigue were familiar to him; yet he often failed in his most deep-laid designs, at the very moment of their apparent success, by the recoil of the bad faith and treachery with which his plans were overcharged.

Such was the man who now began that terrible reign which menaced utter ruin to the national prosperity of the Netherlands. His father had already sapped its foundations, by encouraging foreign manners and ideas among the nobility, and dazzling them with the hope of the honours and wealth which he had at his disposal abroad. His severe edicts against heresy had also begun to accustom the nation to religious discords and hatred. Philip soon enlarged on what Charles had commenced, and he unmercifully sacrificed the well-being of a people to the worst objects of. his selfish ambition.

Philip had only once visited the Netherlands before his accession to sovereign power. Being at that time twenty-two years of age, his opinions were formed and his prejudices deeply rooted. Everything that he observed on this visit was calculated to revolt both. The frank cordiality of the people appeared too familiar. The expression of popular rights sounded like the voice of rebellion. Even the magnificence displayed in his honour offended his jealous vanity. From that moment he seems to have conceived an implacable aversion to the country, in which alone, of all his vast possessions, he could not display the power or inspire the terror of despotism.

The sovereign's dislike was fully equalled by the disgust of his subjects. His haughty severity and vexatious etiquette revolted their pride as well as their plain dealing; and the moral qualities of their new sovereign were considered with loathing. The commercial and political connexion between the Netherlands and Spain had given the two people ample opportunities for mutual acquaintance. The dark, vindictive dispositions of the latter inspired a deep antipathy in those whom civilization had softened and liberty rendered frank and generous; and the new sovereign seemed to embody all that was repulsive and odious in the nation of which he was the type. Yet Philip did not at first act in a way to make himself more particularly hated. He rather, by an apparent consideration for a few points of political interest and individual privilege, and particularly by the revocation of some of the edicts against heretics, removed the suspicions his earlier conduct had excited; and his intended victims did not perceive that the despot sought to lull them to sleep, in the hopes of making them an easier prey.

Philip knew well that force alone was insufficient to reduce such a people to slavery. He succeeded in persuading the states to grant him considerable subsidies, some of which were to be paid by instalments during a period of nine years. That was gaining a great step towards his designs, as it superseded the necessity of a yearly application to the three orders, the guardians of the public liberty. At the same time, he sent secret agents to Rome, to obtain the approbation of the pope to his insidious but most effective plan for placing the whole of the clergy in dependence upon the crown. He also kept up the army of Spaniards and Germans which his father had formed on the frontiers of France; and although he did not remove from their employments the functionaries already in place, he took care to make no new appointments to office among the natives of the Netherlands.

In the midst of these cunning preparations for tyranny, Philip was suddenly attacked in two quarters at once; by Henry II. of France, and by Pope Paul IV. A prince less obstinate than Philip would in such circumstances have renounced, or at least postponed, his designs against the liberties of so important a part of his dominions, as those to which he was obliged to have recourse for aid in support of this double war. But he seemed to make every foreign consideration subservient to the object of domestic aggression which he had so much at heart.

He, however, promptly met the threatened dangers from abroad. He turned his first attention towards his contest with the pope; and he extricated himself from it with an adroitness that proved the whole force and cunning of his character. Having first publicly obtained the opinion of several doctors of theology, that he was justified in taking arms against the pontiff (a point on which there was really no doubt,) he prosecuted the war with the utmost vigour, by the means of the afterwards notorious Duke of Alva, at that time viceroy of his Italian dominions. Paul soon yielded to superior skill and force, and demanded terms of peace, which were granted with a readiness and seeming liberality that astonished no one more than the defeated pontiff. But Philip's moderation to his enemy was far outdone by his perfidy to his allies. He confirmed Alva's consent to the confiscation of the domains of the noble Romans who had espoused his cause; and thus, gained a staunch and powerful supporter to all his future projects in the religious authority of the successor of St Peter.

His conduct in the conclusion of the war with France was not less base. His army, under the command of Philibert Emmanuel, Duke of Savoy, consisting of Belgians, Germans, and Spaniards, with a considerable body of English, sent by Mary to the assistance of her husband, penetrated into Picardy, and gained a complete victory over the French forces. The honour of this brilliant affair, which took place near St Quintin, was almost wholly due to the Count d'Egmont, a Belgian noble, who commanded the light cavalry; but the king, unwilling to let any one man enjoy the glory of the day, piously pretended that he owed the entire obligation to St Lawrence, on whose festival the battle was fought His gratitude or hypocrisy found a fitting monument in the celebrated convent and palace of the Escurial, which he absurdly caused to be built in the form of a gridiron, the instrument of the saint's martyrdom. When the news of the victory reached Charles V. in his retreat, the old warrior inquired if Philip was in Parish but the cautious victor had no notion of such prompt manoeuvring; nor would he risk against foreign enemies the exhaustion of forces destined for the enslavement of his people.

The French in some measure retrieved their late disgrace by the capture of Calais, the only town remaining to England of all its French conquests, and which, consequently, had deeply interested the national glory of each people. In the early part of the year 1558, one of the generals of Henry II. made an irruption into Western Flanders; but the gallant Count of Egmont once more proved his valour and skill, by attacking and totally defeating the invaders near the town of Gravelines.

A general peace was concluded in April, 1559, which bore the name of Câteau-Cambresis, from that of the place where it was negotiated. Philip secured for himself various advantages in the treaty; but he sacrificed the interests of England, by consenting to the retention of Calais by the French king—a cession deeply humiliating to the national pride of his allies; and, if general opinion be correct, a proximate cause of his consort's death. The alliance of France and the support of Rome, the important results of the two wars now brought to a close, were counterbalanced by the well-known hostility of Elizabeth, who had succeeded to the throne of England; and this latter consideration was an additional motive with Philip to push forward the design of consolidating his despotism in the Low Countries.

To lead his already deceived subjects the more surely into the snare, he announced his intended departure on a short visit to Spain; and created for the period of his absence a provisional government, chiefly composed of the leading men among the Belgian nobility. He flattered himself that the states, dazzled by the illustrious illusion thus prepared, would cheerfully grant to this provisional government the right of levying taxes during the temporary absence of the sovereign. He also reckoned on the influence of the clergy in the national assembly, to procure the revival of the edicts against heresy, which he had gained the merit of suspending. These, with many minor details of profound duplicity, formed the principal features of a plan, which, if successful, would have reduced the Netherlands to the wretched state of colonial dependence by which Naples, and Sicily were held in the tenure of Spain.

As soon as the states had consented to place the whole powers of government in the hands of the new administration for the period of the king's absence, the royal hypocrite believed his scheme secure, and flattered himself he had established an instrument of durable despotism. The composition of this new government was a masterpiece of political machinery. It consisted of several councils, in which the most distinguished citizens were entitled to a place, in sufficient numbers to deceive the people with a show of representation, but not enough to command a majority, which was sure on any important question to rest with the titled creatures of the court. The edicts against heresy, soon adopted, gave to the clergy an almost unlimited power over the lives and fortunes of the people. But almost all the dignitaries of the church being men of great respectability and moderation, chosen by the body of the inferior clergy, these extraordinary powers excited little alarm. Philip's project was suddenly to replace these virtuous ecclesiastics by others of his own choice, as soon as the states broke up from their annual, meeting; and for this intention he had procured the secret consent and authority of the court of Rome.

In support of these combinations, the Belgian troops were completely broken up and scattered in small bodies over the country. The whole of this force, so redoubtable to the fears of despotism, consisted of only 3000 cavalry. It was now divided into fourteen companies (or squadrons in the modem phraseology,) under the command of as many independent chiefs, so as to leave little chance of any principle of union reigning among them. But the German and Spanish troops in Philip's pay were cantoned on the frontiers, ready to stifle any incipient effort in opposition to his plans. In addition to these imposing means for their execution, he had secured a still more secret and more powerful support—a secret article in the treaty of Câteau-Cambresis obliged the king of France to assist him with the whole armies of France against his Belgian subjects, should they prove refractory. Thus, the late war, of which the Netherlands had borne all the weight, and earned all the glory, only brought about the junction of the defeated enemy with their own king for the extinction of their national independence.

To complete the execution of this system of perfidy, Philip convened an assembly of all the states at Ghent, in the month of July, 1559. This meeting of the representatives of the three orders of the state offered no apparent obstacle to Philip's views. The clergy, alarmed at the progress of the new doctrines, gathered more closely round the government of which they required the support. The nobles had lost much of their ancient attachment to liberty; and had become, in various ways, dependent on the royal favour. Many of the first families were then represented by men possessed rather of courage and candour than of foresight and sagacity. That of Nassau, the most distinguished of all, seemed the least interested in the national cause. A great part of its possessions were in Germany and France, where it had recently acquired the sovereign principality of Orange. It was only from the third order—that of the commons—that Philip had to expect any opposition. Already, during the war, it had shown some discontent, and had insisted on the nomination of commissioners to control the accounts and the disbursements of the subsidies. But it seemed improbable, that among this class of men, any would be found capable of penetrating the manifold combinations of the king, and disconcerting his designs.

Anthony Perrenotte de Granvelle, Bishop of Arras, who was considered as Philip's favourite counsellor, but who was in reality no more than his docile agent, was commissioned to address the assembly in the name of his master, who spoke only Spanish. His oration was one of cautious deception and contained the most flattering assurances of Philip's attachment to the people of the Netherlands. It excused the king for not having nominated his only son Don Carlos to reign over them in his name; alleging, as a proof of his royal affection, that he preferred giving them as government a Belgian princess, Madame Marguerite Duchess of Parma, the natural daughter of Charles V. by a young lady a native of Audenarde. Fair promises and fine words were thus lavished in profusion to gain the confidence of the deputies.

But notwithstanding all the talent, the caution, and the mystery of Philip and his minister, there was among the nobles one man who saw through all. This individual, endowed with many of the highest attributes of political genius, and pre-eminently, with judgment, the most important of all, entered fearlessly into the contest against tyranny—despising every personal sacrifice for the country's good. Without making himself suspiciously prominent, he privately warned some members of the states of the coming danger. Those in whom he confided did not betray the trust. They spread among the other deputies the alarm, and pointed out the danger to which they had been so judiciously awakened. The consequence was, a reply to Philip's demand, in vague and general terms, without binding the nation by any pledge; and an unanimous entreaty that he would diminish the taxes, withdraw the foreign troops, and entrust no official employments to any but natives of the country. The object of this last request was the removal of Granvelle, who was born in Franche-Comté.

Philip was utterly astounded at all this. In the first moment of his vexation he imprudently cried out, "Would ye, then, also bereave *me* of my place; I, who am a Spaniard?" But he soon recovered his self-command, and resumed his usual mask; expressed his regret at not having sooner learned the wishes of the state; promised to remove the foreign troops within three months; and set off for Zealand, with assumed composure, but filled with the fury of a discovered traitor and a humiliated despot

A fleet under the command of Count Horn, the admiral of the United Provinces, waited at Flessingue to form his escort to Spain. At the very moment of his departure, William of Nassau, Prince of Orange and Governor of Zealand, waited on him to pay his official respects. The king, taking him apart from the other attendant nobles, recommended him to hasten the execution of several gentlemen and wealthy citizens attached to the newly introduced religious opinions. Then, quite suddenly, whether in the random impulse of suppressed rage, or that his piercing glance discovered William's secret feelings in his countenance, he accused him with having been the means of thwarting his designs.

"Sire," replied Nassau, "it was the work of the national states."

"No!" cried Philip, grasping him furiously by the arm; "it was not done by the states, but by you, and you alone!" (Schiller. The words of Philip were: "*No, no los estados; ma vos, vos, vos!*" *Vos* thus used in Spanish is a term of contempt, equivalent to *toi* in French.)

This glorious accusation was not repelled. He who had saved his country in unmasking the designs of its tyrant, admitted by his silence his title to the hatred of the one and the gratitude of the other. On the 20th of August, Philip embarked and set sail; turning his back forever on the country which offered the first check to his despotism; and, after a perilous voyage, he arrived in that which permitted a free indulgence to his ferocious and sanguinary career.

For some time after Philip's departure, the Netherlands continued to enjoy considerable prosperity. From the period of the peace of Câteau-Cambresis, commerce and navigation had acquired new and increasing activity. The fisheries, but particularly that of herrings, became daily more important; that one alone occupying 2000 boats. While Holland, Zealand, and Friesland made this progress in their peculiar branches at industry, the southern provinces were not less active or successful. Spain and the colonies offered such a mart for the objects of their manufacture, that in a single year they received from Flanders fifty large ships, filled with articles of household furniture and utensils. The exportation of woollen goods amounted to enormous sums. Bruges alone sold annually to the amount of 4,000,000 florins of stuffs of Spanish, and as much of English, wool; and the least value of the florin then was quadruple its present worth.

The commerce with England though less important than that with Spain, was calculated yearly at 24,000,000 florins, which was chiefly clear profit to the Netherlands, as their exportations consisted almost entirely of objects of their own manufacture. Their commercial relations with France, Germany, Italy, Portugal, and the Levant, were daily increasing. Antwerp was the centre of this prodigious trade. Several sovereigns, among others Elizabeth of England, had recognised agents in that city, equivalent to consuls of the present times; and loans of immense amount were frequently negotiated by them with wealthy merchants, who furnished them, not in negotiable bills or for unredeemable debentures, but in solid gold, and on a simple acknowledgment.

Flanders and Brabant were still the richest and most flourishing portions of the state. Some municipal *fêtes* given about this time afford a notion of their opulence. On one of these occasions the town of Mechlin sent a deputation to Antwerp, consisting of 326 horsemen dressed in velvet and satin with gold and silver ornaments; while those of Brussels consisted of 340, as splendidly equipped, and accompanied by seven huge triumphal chariots and seventy-eight carriages of various constructions—a prodigious number for those days.

But the splendour and prosperity which thus sprung out of the national industry and independence, and which a wise or a generous sovereign would have promoted, or at least have established on a permanent basis, was destined speedily to sink beneath the bigoted fury of Philip II. The new government which he had established was most ingeniously adapted to produce every imaginable evil to the state. The king, hundreds of leagues distant, could not himself issue an order but with a lapse of time ruinous to any object of pressing importance. The *governant*-general, who represented him, having but a nominal authority, was forced to follow her instructions, and liable to have all her acts reversed, (Vandervynct); besides which, she had the king's orders to consult her private council on all affairs whatever, and the council of state on any matter of paramount importance. These two councils, however, contained the elements of a serious opposition to the royal projects, in the persons of the patriot nobles sprinkled among Philip's devoted creatures.

Thus, the influence of the crown was often thwarted, if not actually balanced; and the proposals which emanated from it frequently opposed by the *governant* herself. She, although a woman of masculine appearance and habits (Strada), was possessed of no strength of mind. Her prevailing sentiment seemed to be dread of the king; yet she was at times influenced by a sense of justice, and by the remonstrances of the well-judging members of her councils. But these were not all the difficulties that clogged the machinery of the state. After the king, the government, and the councils, had deliberated on any measure, its execution rested with the provincial governors or *stadtholders*, or the magistrates of the towns. Almost every one of these, being strongly attached to the laws and customs of the nation, hesitated, or refused to obey the orders conveyed to them, when those orders appeared illegal. Some, however, yielded to the authority of the government; so, it often happened that an edict, which in one district was carried into full effect, was in others deferred, rejected, or violated, in a way productive of great confusion in the public affairs.

Philip was conscious that he had himself to blame for the consequent disorder. In nominating the members of the two councils, he had overreached himself in his plan for silently sapping the liberty that was so obnoxious to his designs. But to neutralise the influence of the restive members, he had left Granvelle the first place in the administration. This man, an immoral ecclesiastic, an eloquent orator, a supple courtier, and a profound politician, bloated with pride, envy, insolence, and vanity, (Strada), was the real head of the government.

Next to him among the royalist party was Viglius, president of the privy-council, an erudite schoolman, attached less to the broad principles of justice than to the letter of the laws, and thus carrying pedantry into the very councils of the state. Next in order came the Count de Berlaimont, head of the financial department—a stern and intolerant satellite of the court, and a furious enemy to those national institutions which operated as checks upon fraud. These three individuals formed the *governant's* privy-council. The remaining creatures of the king were mere subaltern agents.

A government so composed could scarcely fail to excite discontent, and create danger to the public weal. The first proof of incapacity was elicited by the measures required for the departure of the Spanish troops. The period fixed by the king had already expired, and these oboxious foreigners were still in the country, living in part on pillage, and each day committing some new excess. Complaints were carried in successive gradation from the government to the council, and from the council to the king. The Spaniards were removed to Zealand; but instead of being embarked at any of its ports, they were detained there on various pretexts. Money, ships, or, on necessity, a wind, was professed to be still wanting for their final removal, by those who found excuses for delay in every element of nature or subterfuge of art. In the meantime, those ferocious soldiers ravaged a part of the country. The simple natives at length declared they would open the sluices of their dikes; preferring to be swallowed by the waters rather than remain exposed to the cruelty and rapacity of those Spaniards. (Watson's *Life of Philip II.*) Still the embarkation was postponed; until the king, requiring his troops in Spain for some domestic project, they took their long-desired departure in the beginning of the year 1561.

The public discontent at this just cause was soon, however, overwhelmed by one infinitely more important and lading. The Belgian clergy had hitherto formed a free and powerful order in the state, governed and represented by four bishops, chosen by the chapters of the towns, or elected by the monks of the principal abbeys. These bishops, possessing an independent territorial revenue, and not directly subject to the influence of the crown, had interests and feelings in common with the nation. But Philip had prepared, and the pope had sanctioned, the new system of ecclesiastical organisation before alluded to, and the provisional government now put it into execution. (Vandervynct.) Instead of four bishops, it was intended to appoint eighteen, their nomination being vested in the king.

By a wily system of trickery, the subserviency of the abbeys was also aimed at. The new prelates, on a pretended principle of economy, were endowed with the title of abbots of the chief monasteries of their respective dioceses. Thus, not only would they enjoy the immense wealth of these establishments, but the political rights of the abbots whom they were to succeed; and the whole of the ecclesiastical order become gradually represented (after the death of the then living abbots) by the creatures of the crown.

The consequences of this vital blow to the integrity of the national institutions were evident; and the indignation of both clergy and laity was universal. Every legal means of opposition were resorted to, but the people were without leaders; the states were not in session. While the authority of the pope and the king combined, the reverence excited by the very name of religion, and the address and perseverance of the government, formed too powerful a combination, and triumphed over the national discontents which had not yet been formed into resistance. The new bishops were appointed; Granvelle securing for himself the archiepiscopal see of Mechlin, with the title of primate of the Low Countries. At the same time Paul IV. put the crowning point to the capital of his ambition, by presenting him with a cardinal's hat.

The new bishops were to a man most violent, intolerant, and it may be conscientious, opponents to the wide-spreading doctrines of reform. The execution of the edicts against heresy was confided to them. The provincial governors and inferior magistrates were commanded to aid them with a strong arm; and the most unjust and frightful persecution immediately commenced. But still some of these governors and magistrates, considering themselves not only the officers of the prince, but the protectors of the people, and the defenders of the laws rather than of the faith, did not blindly conform to those harsh and illegal commands. The Prince of Orange, *Stadtholder* of Holland, Zealand, and Utrecht, and the Count of Egmont, Governor of Flanders and Artois, permitted no persecutions in those five provinces. But in various places the very people, even when influenced by their superiors, openly opposed it Catholics as well as Protestants were indignant, at the atrocious spectacles of cruelty presented on all sides. The public peace was endangered by isolated acts of resistance, and fears of a general insurrection soon became universal.

The apparent temporising or seeming uncertainty of the champions of the new doctrines formed the great obstacle to the reformation, and tended to prolong the dreadful struggle which was now only commencing, in the Low Countries. It was a matter of great difficulty to convince the people that popery was absurd, and at the same time to set limits to the absurdity. Had the change been from blind belief to total infidelity, it would (as in a modern instance) have been much easier, though less lasting. Men might, in a time of such excitement, have been persuaded that *all* religion productive of abuses such as then abounded was a farce, and that common sense called for its abolition.

But when the boundaries of belief became a question; when the world was told it ought to reject some doctrines, and retain others which seemed as difficult of comprehension; when one tenet was pronounced idolatry, and to doubt another declared damnation—the world either exploded or recoiled: it went too far, or it shrank back; plunged into atheism, or relapsed into popery. It was thus the reformation was checked in the first instance. Its supporters were the strong-minded, and intelligent; and they never, and least of all in those days, formed the mass. Superstition and bigotry had enervated the intellects of the majority; and the high resolve of those with whom the great work commenced, was mixed with a severity that materially retarded its progress. For though personal interests, as with Henry VIII. of England, and rigid enthusiasm, as with Calvin, strengthened the infant reformation; the first led to violence which irritated many, the second to austerity which disgusted them; and it was soon discovered that the change was almost confined to forms of practice, and that the essentials of abuse were likely to be carefully preserved. All these, and other arguments, artfully modified to distract the people, were urged by the new bishops in the Netherlands, and by those whom they employed to arrest the progress of reform.

Among the various causes of the general confusion, the situation of Brabant gave to that province a peculiar share of suffering. Brussels, its capital, being the seat of government, had no particular chief magistrate, like the other provinces. The executive power was therefore wholly confided to the municipal authorities and the territorial proprietors. But these, though generally patriotic in their views, were divided into a multiplicity of different opinions. Rivalry and resentment produced a total want of union, ended in anarchy, and prepared the way for civil war. William of Nassau penetrated the cause, and proposed the remedy in moving for the appointment of a provincial governor. This proposition terrified Granvelle, who saw, as clearly as did his sagacious opponent in the council, that the nomination of a special protector between the people and the government would have paralyzed all his efforts for hurrying on the discord and resistance which were meant to be the plausible excuses for the introduction of arbitrary power.

He therefore energetically dissented from the proposed measure, and William immediately desisted from his demand. But he at the same time claimed, in the name of the whole country, the convocation of the states-general. This assembly alone was competent to decide what was just, legal, and obligatory for each province and every town. Governors, magistrates, and simple citizens, would thus have some rule for their common conduct; and the government would be at least endowed with the dignity of uniformity and steadiness. The ministers endeavoured to evade a demand which they were at first unwilling openly to refuse. But the firm demeanour and persuasive eloquence of the Prince of Orange carried before them all who were not actually bought by the crown; and Granvelle found himself at length forced to avow that an express order from the king forbade the convocation of the states, on any pretext, during his absence.

The veil was thus rent asunder, which had in some measure concealed the deformity of Philip's despotism. The result was a powerful confederacy among all who held it odious, for the overthrow of Granvelle, to whom they chose to attribute the king's conduct; thus, bringing into practical result the sound principle of ministerial responsibility, without which, except in some peculiar case of local urgency or political crisis, the name of constitutional government is but a mockery. Many of the royalist nobles united for the national cause; and even the *governant* joined her efforts to theirs, for an object which would relieve her from the tyranny which none felt more than she did. Those who composed this confederacy against the minister were actuated by a great variety of motives. The Duchess of Parma hated him, as a domestic spy robbing her of all real authority; the royalist nobles, as an insolent upstart at every instant mortifying their pride. The Counts Egmont and Horn, with nobler sentiments, opposed him as the author of their country's growing misfortunes. But it is doubtful if any of the confederates except the Prince of Orange clearly saw that they were putting themselves in direct and personal opposition to the king himself William alone, clear-sighted in politics and profound in his views, knew, in thus devoting himself to the public cause, the adversary with whom he entered the lists.

This great man, for whom the national traditions still preserve the sacred title of "father" (*Vader-Willem,*) and who was in truth not merely the parent but the political creator of the country, was at this period in his thirtieth year. He already joined the vigour of manhood to the wisdom, of age. Brought up under the eye of Charles V., whose sagacity soon discovered his precocious talents, he was admitted to the councils of the emperor, at a time of life which was little advanced beyond mere boyhood. He alone was chosen by this powerful sovereign to be present at the audiences which he gave to foreign ambassadors, which proves that in early youth he well deserved by his discretion the surname of "the taciturn." It was on the arm of William, then twenty years of age, and already named by him to the command of the Belgian troops, that this powerful monarch leaned for support on the memorable day of his abdication; and he immediately afterwards employed him on the important mission of bearing the imperial crown to his brother Ferdinand, in whose favour he bad resigned it.

William's grateful attachment to Charles did not blind him to the demerits of Philip. He repaired to France, as one of the hostages on the part of the latter monarch for the fulfilment of the peace of Câteau-Cambresis; and he then learned from the lips of Henry II., who soon conceived a high esteem for him, the measures reciprocally agreed on by the two sovereigns for the oppression of their subjects. (Vandervynct) From that moment his mind was made up on the character of Philip, and on the part which he had himself to perform; and he never felt a doubt on the first point, nor swerved from the latter.

But even before his patriotism was openly displayed, Philip had taken a dislike to one in whom his shrewdness quickly discovered an intellect of which he was jealous. He could not actually remove William from all interference with public affairs; but he refused him the government of Flanders, and opposed, in secret, his projected marriage with a princess of the house of Lorraine, which was calculated to bring him a considerable accession of fortune, and consequently of influence. It may be therefore said that William, in his subsequent conduct, was urged by motives of personal enmity against Philip. Be it so. We do not seek to raise him above the common feelings of humanity; and we should risk the sinking him below them, if we supposed him insensible to the natural effects of just resentment

The secret impulses of conduct can never be known beyond the individual's own breast; but actions must, however questionable, be taken as the tests of motives. In all those of William's illustrious career we can detect none that might be supposed to spring from vulgar or base feelings. If his hostility to Philip was indeed increased by private dislike, he has at least set an example of unparalleled dignity in his method of revenge; but in calmly considering and weighing, without deciding on the question, we see nothing that should deprive William of an unsullied title to pure and perfect patriotism. The injuries done to him by Philip at this period were not of a nature to excite any violent hatred. Enough of public wrong was inflicted to arouse the patriot, but not of private ill to inflame the man.

Neither was William of a vindictive disposition. He was never known to turn the knife of an assassin against his royal rival, even when the blade hired by the latter glanced from him reeking with his blood. And though William's enmity may have been kept alive or strengthened by the provocations he received, it is certain that, if a foe to the king, he was, as long as it was possible, the faithful counsellor of the crown. He spared no pains to impress on the monarch who hated him the real means for preventing the coming evils; and had not a revolution been absolutely inevitable, it is he who would have prevented it.

Such was the chief of the patriot party, chosen by the silent election of general opinion, and by that involuntary homage to genius, which leads individuals in the train of those master-minds who take the lead in public affairs. Counts Egmont and Horn, and some others, largely shared with him the popular favour. The multitude could not for some time distinguish the uncertain and capricious opposition of an offended courtier from the determined resistance of a great man. William was still comparatively young; he had lived long out of the country; and it was little by little that his eminent public virtues were developed and understood.

The great object of immediate good was the removal of cardinal Granvelle. William boldly put himself at the head of the confederacy. He wrote to the king, conjointly with counts Egmont and Horn, faithfully portraying the state of affairs. The Duchess of Parma backed this remonstrance with a strenuous request for Granvelle's dismission. Philip's reply to the three noblemen was a mere tissue of duplicity to obtain delay, accompanied by an invitation to Count Egmont to repair to Madrid, to hear his sentiments at large by word of mouth. His only answer to the *governant* was a positive recommendation to use every possible means to disunite and breed ill-will among the three confederate lords.

It was difficult to deprive William of the confidence of his friends, and impossible to deceive him. He saw the trap prepared by the royal intrigues, restrained Egmont for a while from the fatal step he was but too well inclined to take, and persuaded him and Horn to renew with him their firm but respectful representations; at the same time begging permission to resign their various employments, and simultaneously ceasing to appear at the court of the *governant*.

In the meantime, every possible indignity was offered to the cardinal by private pique and public satire. Several lords, following Count Egmont's example, had a kind of *capuchon* or fool's-cap embroidered on the liveries of their varlets; and it was generally known that this was meant as a practical parody on the cardinal's hat. The crowd laughed heartily at this stupid pleasantry; and the coarse satire of the times may be judged by a caricature, which was forwarded to the cardinal's own hands, representing him in the act of hatching a nest full of eggs, from which a crowd of bishops escaped, while overhead was the devil in *propriâ personâ*, with the following scroll:—"This is my well-beloved son—listen to him!" (Dujardin, *Hist. Gen. des Prov. Un.* t. v.)

Philip, thus driven before the popular voice, found himself forced to the choice of throwing off the mask at once, or of sacrificing Granvelle. An invincible inclination for manoeuvring and deceit decided him on the latter measure; and the cardinal, recalled but not disgraced, quitted the Netherlands on the 10th of March, 1564. (Vandervynct.) The secret instructions to the *governant* remained unrevoked; the president Viglius succeeded to the post which Granvelle had occupied; and it was clear that the projects of the king had suffered no change.

Nevertheless, some good resulted from the departure of the unpopular minister. The public fermentation subsided; the patriot lords reappeared at court; and the Prince of Orange acquired an increasing influence in the council and over the *governant*, who by his advice adopted a conciliatory line of conduct—a fallacious but still a temporary hope for the nation. But the calm was of short duration. Scarcely was this moderation evinced by the government, when Philip, obstinate in his designs, and outrageous in his resentment, sent an order to have the edicts against heresy put into most rigorous execution, and to proclaim throughout the seventeen provinces the furious decree of the council of Trent

The revolting cruelty and illegality of the first edicts were already admitted. As to the decrees of this memorable council, they were only adapted for countries in submission to an absolute despotism. They were received in the Netherlands with general reprobation. Even the new bishops loudly denounced them as unjust innovations; and thus, Philip found zealous opponents in those on whom he had reckoned as his most servile tools. The *governant* was not the less urged to implicit obedience to the orders of the king by Viglius and De Berlaimont, who took upon themselves an almost menacing tone. The duchess assembled a council of state, and asked, its advice as to her proceedings. The Prince of Orange at once boldly proposed disobedience to pleasures fraught with danger to the monarchy and ruin to the nation. The council could not resist his appeal to their best feelings. His proposal that fresh remonstrances should be addressed to the king, met with almost general support. The president Viglius, who had spoken in the opening of the council in favour of the kind's orders, was overwhelmed by William's reasoning, and demanded time to prepare his reply. His agitation during the debate, and his despair of carrying the measures against the patriot party, brought on in the night an attack of apoplexy.

It was resolved to dispatch a special envoy to Spain, to explain to Philip the views of the council, and to lay before him a plan proposed by the Prince of Orange for forming a junction between the two councils and that of finance, and forming them into one body. The object of this measure was at once to give greater union and power to the provisional government, to create a central administration in the Netherlands, and to remove from some obscure and avaricious financiers the exclusive management of the national resources. The Count of Egmont, chosen by the council for this important mission, set out for Madrid in the month of February, 1565. Philip received him with profound hypocrisy; loaded him with the most flattering promises; sent him back in the utmost elation: and when the credulous count returned to Brussels, he found that the written orders, of which he was the bearer, were in direct variance with every word which the king had uttered. (Vandervynct.)

These orders were chiefly concerning the, reiterated subject of the persecution to be inflexibly pursued against the religious reformers. Not satisfied with the hitherto established forms of punishment, Philip now expressly commanded that the more revolting means decreed by his father in the rigor of his early zeal, such as burning, living burial, and the like, should be adopted; and he somewhat more obscurely directed that the victims should be no longer publicly immolated, but secretly destroyed. He endeavoured, by this vague phraseology, to avoid, the actual utterance of the word *inquisition*; but he thus virtually established that atrocious tribunal, with attributes still more terrific than even in Spain; for there the condemned had at least the consolation of dying in open day, and of displaying the fortitude which is rarely proof against the horror of a private execution. Philip had thus consummated his treason against the principles of justice and the practices of jurisprudence, which had heretofore characterized the country; and against the most vital of those privileges which he had solemnly sworn to maintain.

His design of establishing this horrible tribunal, so impiously named *holy* by its founders, had been long suspected by the people of the Netherlands. The expression of those fears had reached him more than once. He as often replied by assurances that he had formed no such project, and particularly to Count d'Egmont during his recent visit to Madrid. But at that very time he assembled a conclave of his creatures, doctors of theology, of whom he formally demanded an opinion as to whether he could conscientiously tolerate two sorts of religion in the Netherlands. The doctors, hoping to please him, replied, that "he might, for the avoidance of a greater evil."

Philip trembled with rage, and exclaimed, with a threatening tone, "I ask not if I *can*, but if I *ought*." The theologians read in this question the nature of the expected reply; and it was amply conformable to his wish. He immediately threw himself on his knees before a crucifix, and raising his hands towards heaven, put up a prayer for strength in his resolution to pursue as deadly enemies all who viewed that effigy with feelings different from his own. If this were not really a sacrilegious farce, it must be that the blaspheming bigot believed the Deity to be a monster of cruelty like himself.

Even Viglius was terrified by the nature of Philip's commands; and the patriot lords once more withdrew from all share in the government, leaving to the Duchess of Parma and her ministers the whole responsibility of the new measures. They were at length put into actual and vigourous execution in the beginning of the year 1566. The inquisitors of the faith, with their familiars, stalked abroad boldly in the devoted provinces, carrying persecution and death in their train. Numerous but partial insurrections opposed these odious intruders. Every district and town became the scene of frightful executions or tumultuous resistance. The converts to the new doctrines multiplied, as usual, under the effects of persecution. A contemporary author says:

> There was nowhere to be seen the meanest mechanic who did not find a weapon to strike down the murderers of his compatriots.

Holland, Zealand, and Utrecht, alone escaped from those fast accumulating horrors. William of Nassau was there.

Chapter 2

1566

Commencement of this Revolution

The *governant* and her ministers now began to tremble. Philip's favourite counsellors advised him to yield to the popular despair; but nothing could change his determination to pursue his bloody game to the last chance. He had foreseen the impossibility of reducing the country to slavery as long as it maintained its tranquillity, and that union which forms in itself the elements and the cement of strength. It was from deep calculation that he had excited the troubles, and now kept them alive. He knew that the structure of illegal power could only be raised on the ruins of public rights and national happiness; and the materials of desolation found sympathy in his congenial mind.

And now in reality began the awful revolution of the Netherlands against their tyrant. In a few years this so lately flourishing and happy nation presented a frightful picture; and in the midst of European peace, prosperity, and civilization, the wickedness of one prince drew down on the country he misgoverned more evils than it had suffered for centuries from the worst effects of its foreign foes.

William of Nassau has been accused of having at length urged on the *governant* to promulgate the final edicts and the resolutions of the council of Trent, and then retiring from the council of state. This line of conduct may be safely admitted and fairly defended by his admirers. He had seen the uselessness of remonstrance against the intentions of the king. Every possible means had been tried, without effect, to soften his pitiless heart to the sufferings of the country. At length the moment came when the people had reached that pitch of despair which is the great force of the oppressed, and William felt, that their strength was now equal to the contest he had long foreseen. It is therefore absurd to accuse him of artifice in the exercise of that wisdom which rarely failed him on any important crisis. A change of circumstances gives a new name to actions and motives; and it would be hard to blame William of Nassau for the only point in which he bore the least resemblance to Philip of Spain—that depth of penetration, which the latter turned to every base, and the former to every noble purpose.

Up to the present moment the Prince of Orange and the Counts Egmont and Horn, with their partisans and friends, had sincerely desired the public peace, and acted in the common interest of the king and the people. But all the nobles had not acted with the same constitutional moderation. Many of those, disappointed on personal accounts, others professing the new doctrines, and the rest variously affected by manifold motives, formed a body of violent and sometimes of imprudent malcontents. The marriage of Alexander Prince of Parma, son of the *governant*, which was at this time celebrated at Brussels, brought together an immense number of these dissatisfied nobles, who became thus drawn into closer connexion, and whose national candour was more than usually brought out in the confidential intercourse of society. Politics and patriotism were the common subjects of conversation in the various convivial meetings that took place. Two German nobles, Counts Holle and Schwarzemberg, at that period in the Netherlands, loudly proclaimed the favourable disposition of the princes of the empire towards the Belgians. (Schiller.)

It was supposed even thus early that negotiations had been opened with several of those sovereigns. In short, nothing seemed wanting but a leader, to give consistency and weight to the confederacy which was as yet but in embryo. This was doubly furnished in the persons of Louis of Nassau and Henry de Brederode. The former, brother of the Prince of Orange, was possessed of many of those brilliant qualities which mark men as worthy of distinction in times of peril. Educated at Geneva, he was passionately attached to the reformed religion, and identified in his hatred the Catholic church and the tyranny of Spain. Brave and impetuous, he was, to his elder brother, but as an adventurous partisan compared with a sagacious general. He loved William as well as he did their common cause, and his life was devoted to both.

Henry de Brederode, Lord of Vianen and Marquis of Utrecht, was descended from the ancient counts of Holland. This illustrious origin, which in his own eyes formed a high claim to distinction, had not procured him any of those employments or dignities which he considered his due. He was presumptuous and rash, and rather a fluent speaker than an eloquent orator. Louis of Nassau was thoroughly inspired by the justice of the cause he espoused; De Brederode espoused it for the glory of becoming its champion. The first only wished for action; the latter longed for distinction. But neither the enthusiasm of Nassau, nor the vanity of De Brederode, was allied with those superior, attributes required to form a hero.

The confederation acquired its perfect organisation in the month of February, 1566, on the 10th of which month its celebrated manifesto was signed by its numerous adherents. The first name affixed to this document was that of Philip de Marnix, Lord of St Aldegonde, from whose pen it emanated; a man of great talents both as soldier and writer. Numbers of the nobility followed him on this muster-roll of patriotism, and many of the most zealous royalists were among them. This remarkable proclamation of general feeling consisted chiefly in a powerful reprehension of the illegal establishment of the inquisition in the Low Countries, and a solemn obligation on the members of the confederacy to unite in the common cause against this detested nuisance.

Men of all ranks and classes offered their signatures, and several Catholic priests among the rest. The Prince of Orange, and the Counts Egmont, Horn, and Meghem, declined becoming actual parties to this bold measure; and when the question was debated as to the most appropriate way of presenting an address to the *governant*, these noblemen advised the mildest and most respectful demeanour on the part of the purposed deputation.

At the first intelligence of these proceedings, the Duchess of Parma, absorbed by terror, had no resource but to assemble hastily such members of the council of state as were at Brussels; and She entreated, by the most pressing letters, the Prince of Orange and Count Horn to resume their places at this council. But three courses of conduct seemed applicable to the emergency—to take up arms—to grant the demands of the confederates—or to temporise and to amuse them with a feint of moderation, until the orders of the king might be obtained from Spain. It was not, however, till after a lapse of four months that the council finally met to deliberate on these important questions; and during this long interval at such a crisis, the confederates gained constant accessions to their numbers, and completely consolidated their plans. The opinions in the council were greatly divided as to the mode of treatment towards those, whom one party considered as patriots acting in their constitutional rights, and the other as rebels in open revolt against the king. (Vandervynct.) The Prince of Orange and De Berlaimont were the principal leaders and chief speakers on either side. But the reasonings of the former, backed by the urgency of events, carried the majority of the suffrages; and a promised redress of grievances was agreed on beforehand, as the anticipated answer to the coming demands.

Even while the council of state held its sittings, the report was spread through Brussels that the confederates were approaching. And at length they did enter the city, to the amount of some hundreds of the representatives of the first families in the country. On the following day, the 5th of April, 1566, they walked in solemn procession to the palace. Their demeanour was highly imposing, from their mingled air of forbearance and determination. All Brussels thronged out, to gaze and sympathize with this extraordinary spectacle, of men whose resolute step showed they were no common suppliants, but whose modest bearing had none of the seditious air of faction. The *governant* received the distinguished petitioners with courtesy, listened to their detailed grievances, and returned a moderate, conciliatory, but evasive answer.

The confederation, which owed its birth to, and was cradled in social enjoyments, was consolidated in the midst of a feast. The day following this first deputation to the *governant*, De Brederode gave a grand repast to his associates in the Hôtel de Culembourg. Three hundred guests were present. Inflamed by joy and hope, their spirits rose high under the influence of wine, and temperance gave way to temerity. In the midst of their carousing, some of the members remarked, that when the *governant* received the written petition, Count Berlaimont observed to her, that "she had nothing to fear from such a band of beggars," (*tas de Gueux*.) The fact was, that many of the confederates were, from individual extravagance and mismanagement, reduced to such a state of poverty as to justify in some sort the sarcasm. The chiefs of the company being at that very moment debating on the name which they should choose for this patriotic league, the title of *Gueux* was instantly proposed, and adopted with acclamation.

The reproach it was originally intended to convey became neutralised, as its general application to men of all ranks and fortunes concealed its effect as a stigma on many to whom it might be seriously applied. Neither were examples wanting of the most absurd and apparently dishonouring nicknames being elsewhere adopted by powerful political parties. "Long live the Gueux!" was the toast given and tumultuously drunk by this mad-brained company; and Brederode, setting no bounds to the boisterous excitement which followed, procured immediately, and slung across his shoulders, a wallet such as was worn by pilgrims and beggars; drank to the health of all present, in a wooden cup or porringer; and loudly swore that he was ready to sacrifice his fortune and life for the common cause. Each man passed round the bowl, which he first put to his lips—repeated the oath—and thus pledged himself to the compact. The wallet next went the rounds of the whole assembly, and was finally hung upon a nail driven into the wall for the purpose; and gazed on with such enthusiasm as the emblems of political or religious faith, however worthless or absurd, never fail to inspire in the minds of enthusiasts.

The tumult caused by this ceremony, so ridiculous in itself but so sublime in its results, attracted to the spot the Prince of Orange and Counts Egmont and Horn, whose presence is universally attributed by the historians to accident, but which was probably that kind of chance that leads medical practitioners in our days to the field where a duel is fought. They entered; and Brederode, who did the honours of the mansion, forced them to be seated, and to join in the festivity.

******

The following was Egmont's account of their conduct. "We drank a single glass of wine each, to shouts of 'Long live the king! long live the Gueux!' It was the first time I had heard the confederacy so named, and I avow that it displeased me; but the times were so critical, that people were obliged to tolerate many things contrary to their inclinations, and I believed myself on this occasion to act with perfect innocence."—*Procès criminal du Comte d'Egmont.*

******

The appearance of three such distinguished personages heightened the general excitement; and the most important assemblage that had for centuries met together in the Netherlands mingled the discussion of affairs of state with all the burlesque extravagance of a debauch. But this frantic scene did not finish the affair. What they resolved on while drunk, they prepared to perform when sober. Rallying-signs and watchwords were adopted and soon displayed. It was thought that nothing better suited the occasion than the immediate adoption of the costume as well as the title of beggary. In a very few days the city streets were filled with men in grey cloaks, fashioned on the model of those used by mendicants and pilgrims. Each confederate caused this uniform to be worn by every member of his family, and replaced with it the lively of his servants.

Several fastened to their girdles or their sword-hilts small wooden drinking-cups, clasp-knives, and other symbols of the begging fraternity; while all soon wore on their breasts a medal of gold or silver, representing on one side the effigy of Philip, with the words, "Faithful to the king"; and on the reverse, two hands clasped, with the motto, *"Jusqu' à la besace,"* (Even to the wallet.) From this origin arose the application of the word Gueux, in its political sense, as common to all the inhabitants of the Netherlands who embraced the cause of the Reformation, and took up arms against their tyrant. Having presented two subsequent remonstrances to the *governant*, and obtained some consoling promises of moderation, the chief confederates quitted Brussels, leaving several directors to sustain their cause in the capital; while they themselves spread into the various provinces, exciting the people to join the legal and constitutional resistance with which they were resolved to oppose the march of bigotry and despotism.

A new form of edict was now decided on by the *governant* and her council; and after various insidious and illegal but successful tricks, the consent of several of the provinces was obtained to the adoption of measures that, under a guise of comparative moderation, were little less abominable than those commanded by the king. (Schiller.) These were formally signed by the council, and dispatched to Spain to receive Philip's sanction, and thus acquire the force of law. The embassy to Madrid was confided to the Marquis of Bergen and the Baron de Montigny; the latter of whom was brother to Count Horn, and had formerly been employed on a like mission. Montigny appears to have had some qualms of apprehension in undertaking the new office.

His good genius seemed for a while to stand between him and the fate which awaited him. An accident which happened to his colleague allowed an excuse for retarding his journey. But the *governant* urged him away: he set out, and reached his destination; not to defend the cause of his country at the foot of the throne, but to perish a victim to his patriotism. (Schiller.)

The situation of the patriot lords was at this crisis peculiarly embarrassing. The conduct of the confederates was so essentially tantamount to open rebellion, that the Prince of Orange and his friends found it almost impossible to preserve a neutrality between the court and the people. All their wishes urged them to join at once in the public cause; but they were restrained by a lingering sense of loyalty to the king, whose employments they still held, and whose confidence they were, therefore, nominally supposed to share. They seemed reduced to the necessity of coming to an explanation, and, perhaps, a premature rupture with the government; of joining in the harsh measures it was likely to adopt against those with whose proceedings they sympathized; or, as a last alternative, to withdraw, as they had done before, wholly from all interference in public affairs.

Still their presence in the council of state was, even though their influence had greatly increased, of vast service to the patriots, in checking the hostility of the court; and the confederates, on the other hand, were restrained from acts of open violence, by fear of the disapprobation of these their best and most powerful friends. Be their individual motives or reasoning what they might, they at length, adopted the alternative above alluded to, and resigned their places. Count Horn retired to his estates; Count Egmont repaired to Aix-la-Chapelle, under the pretext of being ordered thither by his physicians; the Prince of Orange remained for a while at Brussels.

In the meanwhile, the confederation gained ground every day. Its measures had totally changed the face of affairs in all parts of the nation. The general discontent now acquired stability, and consequent importance. The chief merchants of many of the towns enrolled themselves in the patriot band. Many active and ardent minds, hitherto withheld by the doubtful construction of the association, now freely entered into it when it took the form of union and respectability. Energy, if not excess, seemed legitimatised. The vanity of the leaders was flattered by the consequence they acquired; and weak minds gladly embraced an occasion of mixing with those whose importance gave both protection and concealment to their insignificance.

An occasion so favourable for the rapid promulgation of the new doctrines was promptly taken advantage of by the French Huguenots and their Protestant brethren of Germany. (Schiller.) The disciples of reform poured from all quarters into the Low Countries, and made prodigious progress, with all the energy of proselytes, and too often with the fury of fanatics. The three principal sects into which the reformers were divided, were those of the Anabaptists, the Calvinists, and the Lutherans. The first and least numerous were chiefly established in Friesland. The second were spread over the eastern provinces. Their doctrines being already admitted into some kingdoms of the north, they were protected by the most powerful princes of the empire. The third, and by far the most numerous and wealthy, abounded in the southern provinces, and particularly in Flanders. They were supported by the zealous efforts of French, Swiss, and German ministers; and their dogmas were nearly the same with those of the established religion of England. The city of Antwerp was the central point of union for the three sects; but the only principle they held in common was their hatred against popery, the inquisition, and Spain.

The *governant* had now issued orders to the chief magistrates to proceed with moderation against the heretics; orders which were obeyed in their most ample latitude by those to whose sympathies they were so congenial. Until then, the Protestants were satisfied to meet by stealth at night; but under this negative protection of the authorities they now boldly assembled in public. Field-preachings commenced in Flanders; and the minister who first set this example was Herman Stricker, a converted monk, a native of Overyssel, a powerful speaker, and a bold enthusiast. He soon drew together an audience of 7000 persons. A furious magistrate rushed among this crowd, and hoped to disperse them sword in hand; but he was soon struck down, mortally wounded, with a shower of stones. (Vandervynct.) Irritated and emboldened by this rash attempt, the Protestants assembled in still greater numbers near Alost; but on this occasion they appeared with poniards, guns, and halberds. They intrenched themselves under the protection of wagons and all sorts of obstacles to a sudden attack; placed outposts and videttes; and thus, took the field in the doubly dangerous aspect of fanaticism and war.

Similar assemblies soon spread over the whole of Flanders, inflamed by the exhortations of Stricker and another preacher, called Peter Dathen, of Poperingue. It was calculated that 15,000 men attended at some of these preachings; while a third apostle of Calvinism, Ambrose Ville, a Frenchman, successfully excited the inhabitants of Tournay, Valenciennes, and Antwerp, to form a common league for the promulgation of their faith. The sudden appearance of De Brederode at the latter place decided their plan, and gave the courage to fix on a day for its execution. An immense assemblage simultaneously quitted the three cities at a preconcerted time; and when they united their forces at the appointed rendezvous, the preachings, exhortations, and psalm-singing commenced, under the auspices of several Huguenot and German ministers, and continued for several days in all the zealous extravagance which may be well imagined to characterize such a scene.

The citizens of Antwerp were terrified for the safety of the place, and courier after courier was dispatched to the *governant* at Brussels to implore her presence. The duchess, not daring to take such a step without the authority of the king, sent Count Meghem as her representative, with proposals to the magistrates to call out the garrison. The populace soon understood the object of this messenger; and assailing him with a violent outcry, forced him to fly from the city. Then the Calvinists petitioned the magistrates for permission to openly exercise their religion, and for the grant of a temple in which to celebrate its rites. The magistrates in this conjuncture renewed their application to the *governant*, and entreated her to send the Prince of Orange, as the only person capable of saving the city from destruction.

The duchess was forced to adopt this bitter alternative; and the prince, after repeated refusals to mix again in public affairs, yielded, at length, less to the supplications of the *governant* than to his own wishes to do another service to the cause of his country. At half a league from the city he was met by De Brederode, with an immense concourse of people of all sects and opinions, who hailed him as a protector from the tyranny of the king, and a saviour from the dangers of their own excess. Nothing could exceed the wisdom, the firmness, and the benevolence, with which he managed all conflicting interests, and preserved tranquillity amidst a chaos of opposing prejudices and passions.

From the first establishment of the field-preachings the *governant* had implored the confederate lords to aid her for the re-establishment of order. De Brederode seized this excuse for convoking a general meeting of the associates, which consequently took place at the town of St, Trond, in the district of Liege. Full 2000 of the members appeared on the summons. The language held in this assembly was much stronger and less equivocal than that formerly used. (Vandervynct.) The delay in the arrival of the king's answer presaged ill as to his intentions; while the rapid growth of the public power seemed to mark the present as the time for successfully demanding all that the people required. Several of the Catholic members, still royalists at heart, were shocked to hear a total liberty of conscience spoken of as one of the privileges sought for. (Schiller.) The young Count of Mansfield, among others, withdrew immediately from the confederation; and thus, the first stone seemed to be removed from this imperfectly constructed edifice.

The Prince of Orange and Count Egmont were applied to, and appointed by the *governant*, with full powers to treat with the confederates. Twelve of the latter, among whom were Louis of Nassau, De Brederode, and De Culembourg, met them by appointment at Duffle, a village not far from Mechlin. The result of the conference was a respectful but firm address to the *governant*, repelling her accusations of having entered into foreign treaties; declaring their readiness to march against the French troops, should they set foot in the country; and claiming, with the utmost force of reasoning, the convocation of the states-general. This was replied to by an entreaty that they would still wait patiently for twenty-four days, in hopes of an answer from the king; and she sent the Marquess of Bergen in all speed to Madrid, to support Montigny in his efforts to obtain some prompt decision from Philip. (Vandervynct.)

The king, who was then at Segovia, assembled his council, consisting of the Duke of Alva and eight other *grandees*. The two deputies from the Netherlands attended at the deliberations, which were held for several successive days; but the king was never present. The whole state of affairs being debated with what appears a calm and dispassionate view, considering the hostile prejudices of this council, it was decided to advise the king to adopt generally a more moderate line of conduct in the Netherlands, and to abolish the inquisition; at the same time prohibiting under the most awful threats all confederation, assemblage, or public preachings, under any pretext whatever. (Schiller.)

The king's first care on receiving this advice was to order, in all the principal towns of Spain and the Netherlands, prayer and processions to implore the divine approbation on the resolutions which he had formed. He appeared then in person at the council of state, and issued a decree, by which he refused his consent to the convocation of the states-general, and bound himself to take several German regiments into his pay. He ordered the Duchess of Parma, by a private letter, to immediately cause to be raised 3000 cavalry and 10,000 foot, and he remitted to her for this purpose 300,000 florins in gold. He next wrote with his own hand to several of his partisans in the various towns, encouraging them in their fidelity to his purposes, and promising them his support. He rejected the adoption of the moderation recommended to him; but he consented to the abolition of the inquisition in its most odious sense, re-establishing that modified species of ecclesiastical tyranny which had been introduced into the Netherlands by Charles V.

The people of that devoted country were thus successful in obtaining one important concession from the king, and in meeting unexpected consideration from this Spanish council. Whether these measures had been calculated with a view to their future, it is not now easy to determine; at all events they came too late. (Vandervynct.) When Philip's letters reached Brussels, the iconoclasts or image-breakers were abroad. (Schiller.)

It requires no profound research to comprehend the impulse which leads a horde of fanatics to the most monstrous excesses. That the deeds of the iconoclasts arose from the spontaneous outburst of mere vulgar fury, admits of no doubt. The aspersion which would trace those deeds to the meeting of St Trend, and fix the infamy on the body of nobility there assembled, is scarcely worthy of refutation. The very lowest of the people were the actors as well as the authors of the outrages, which were at once shocking to every friend of liberty, and injurious to that sacred cause. Artois and western Flanders were the scenes of the first exploits of the iconoclasts.

A band of peasants, intermixed with beggars and various other vagabonds, to the amount of about 300, (Vandervynct), urged by fanaticism and those baser passions which animate every lawless body of men, armed with hatchets, clubs, and hammers, forced open the doors of some of the village churches in the neighbourhood of St Omer, and tore down and destroyed not only the images and relics of saints, but those very ornaments which Christians of all sects hold sacred, and essential to the most simple rites of religion.

The cities of Ypres, Lille, and other places of importance, were soon subject to similar visitations; and the whole of Flanders was in a few days ravaged by furious multitudes, whose frantic energy spread terror and destruction on their route. Antwerp was protected for a while by the presence of the Prince of Orange; but an order from the *governant* having obliged him to repair to Brussels, a few nights after his departure the celebrated cathedral shared the fate of many a minor temple, and was utterly pillaged. The blind fury of the spoilers was not confined to the mere effigies which they considered the types of idolatry, nor even to the pictures, the vases, the sixty-six altars, and their richly wrought accessories; but it was equally fatal to the splendid organ, which was considered the finest at that time in existence.

The rapidity and the order with which this torchlight scene was acted, without a single accident among the numerous doers, has excited the wonder of almost all its early historians. One of them does not hesitate to ascribe the "miracle" to the absolute agency of demons. (Strada.) For three days and nights these revolting scenes were acted, and every church in the city shared the fate of the cathedral, which next to St. Peter's at Rome was the most magnificent in Christendom. (Schiller.)

Ghent, Tournay, Valenciennes, Mechlin, and other cities, were next the theatres of similar excesses; and in an incredibly short space of time above 400 churches were pillaged in Flanders and Brabant Zealand, Utrecht, and others of the northern provinces, suffered more or less; Friesland, Guelders, and Holland alone escaped, and even the latter but in partial instances.

These terrible scenes extinguished every hope of reconciliation with the king. An inveterate and interminable hatred was now established between him and the people; for the whole nation was identified with deeds, which were in reality only shared by the most base, and were loathsome to all who were enlightened. It was in vain that the patriot nobles might hope or strive to exculpate themselves; they were sure to be held criminal either in fact or by implication. No show of loyalty, no efforts to restore order, no personal sacrifice, could save them from the hatred or screen them from the vengeance of Philip.

The affright of the *governant* during the short reign of anarchy and terror was without bounds. She strove to make her escape from Brussels, and was restrained from so doing only by the joint solicitations of Viglius and the various knights of the order of the Golden Fleece, consisting of the first among the nobles of all parties. But, in fact, a species of violence was used to restrain her from this most fatal step; for Viglius gave orders that the gates of the city should be shut, and egress refused to anyone belonging to the court. (Schiller.) The somewhat less terrified duchess now named Count Mansfield governor of the town, reinforced the garrison, ordered arms to be distributed to all her adherents, and then called a council to deliberate on the measures to be adopted.

A compromise with the confederates and the reformers was unanimously agreed to. The Prince of Orange and Counts Egmont and Horn were once more appointed to this arduous arbitration between the court and the people. (Vandervynct.) Necessity now extorted almost every concession which had been so long denied to justice and prudence. The confederates were declared absolved from all responsibility relative to their proceedings. The suppression of the inquisition, the abolition of the edicts against heresy, and a permission for the preachings, were simultaneously published.

The confederates, on their side, undertook to remain faithful to the service of the king, to do their best for the establishment of order, and to punish the iconoclasts. A regular treaty to this effect was drawn up and executed by the respective plenipotentiaries, and formally approved by the *governant*, who affixed her sign-manual to the instrument She only consented to this measure after a long struggle, and with tears in her eyes; and it was with a trembling hand that she wrote an account of these transactions to the king. (Schiller.)

Soon after this the several governors repaired to their respective provinces, and their efforts for the re-establishment of tranquillity were attended with various degrees of success. Several of the ringleaders in the late excesses were executed; and this severity was not confined to the partisans of the Catholic church. The Prince of Orange and Count Egmont, with others of the patriot lords, set the example of this just severity. John Casambrot. Lord of Beckerzeel, Egmont's secretary, and a leading member of the confederation, put himself at the head of some others of the associated gentlemen, fell upon a refractory, band of iconoclasts near Grammont, in Flanders, and took thirty prisoners, of whom he ordered twenty-eight to be hanged on the spot.

CHAPTER 3

1566–1573

TO THE ADMINISTRATION OF REQUESENS

All the services just related in the common cause of the country and the king produced no effect on the vindictive spirit of the latter. Neither the lapse of time, the proofs of repentance, nor the fulfilment of their duty, could efface the hatred excited by a conscientious opposition to even one design of despotism. (Schiller.)

Philip was ill at Segovia when he received accounts of the excesses of the image-breakers, and of the convention concluded with the heretics. (Hopper.) Despatches from the *governant*, with private advices from Viglius, Egmont, Mansfield, Meghem, de Berlaimont, and others, gave him ample information as to the real state of things, and they thus strove to palliate their having acceded to the convention. The emperor even wrote to his royal nephew, imploring him to treat his wayward subjects with moderation, and offered his mediation between them. Philip, though severely suffering, gave great attention to the details of this correspondence, which he minutely examined, and laid before his council of state, with notes and observations taken by himself. But he took special care to send to them only such parts as he chose them to be well informed upon; his natural district not suffering him to have any confidential communication with men. (Hopper.)

Again, the Spanish council appears to have interfered between the people of the Netherlands and the enmity of the monarch; and the offered mediation of the emperor was recommended to his acceptance, to avoid the appearance of a forced concession to the popular will. Philip was also strongly urged to repair to the scene of the disturbances; and a main question of debate was, whether he should march at the head of an army or confide himself to the loyalty and good faith of his Belgian subjects. But the indolence or the pride of Philip was too strong to admit of his taking so vigourous a measure; and all these consultations ended in two letters to the *governant* In the first he declared his firm intention to visit the Netherlands in person; refused to convoke the states-general; passed in silence the treaties concluded with the Protestants and the confederates; and finished by a declaration that he would throw himself wholly on the fidelity of the country. In his second letter, meant for the *governant* alone, he authorised her to assemble the states-general if public opinion became too powerful for resistance, but on no account to let it transpire that he had under any circumstances given his consent

During these deliberations in Spain, the Protestants in the Netherlands amply availed themselves of the privileges they had gained. They erected numerous wooden churches with incredible activity. (Vandervynct.) Young and old, noble and plebeian, of these energetic men, assisted in the manual labours of these occupations; and the women freely applied the produce of their ornaments and jewels to forward the pious work. (Schiller.) But the furious outrages of the iconoclasts had done infinite mischief to both political and religious freedom: many of the Catholics, and particularly the priests, gradually withdrew themselves from the confederacy, which thus lost some of its most firm supporters. And on the other hand, the severity with which some of its members pursued the guilty, offended and alarmed the body of the people, who could not distinguish the shades of difference between the love of liberty and the practice of licentiousness.

The *governant* and her satellites adroitly took advantage of this state of things to sow dissension among the patriots. Autograph letters from Philip to the principal lords were distributed among them with such artful and mysterious precautions, as to throw the rest into perplexity, and give each suspicions of the other's fidelity. The report of the immediate arrival of Philip had also considerable effect over the less resolute, or more selfish; and the confederation was dissolving rapidly under the operations of intrigue, self-interest, and fear. Even the Count of Egmont was not proof against the subtle seductions of the wily monarch, whose severe yet flattering letters half frightened and half soothed him into a relapse of royalism. But with the Prince of Orange Philip had no chance of success. It is unquestionable, that be his means of acquiring information what they might, he did succeed in procuring minute intelligence of all that was going on in the king's most secret council.

He had from time to time procured copies of the *governant's* dispatches; but the document which threw the most important light upon the real intentions of Philip, was a confidential epistle to the *governant* from D'Alava, the Spanish minister at Paris, in which he spoke in terms too clear to admit any doubt as to the terrible example which the king was resolved to make among the patriot lords. (Schiller.) Bergen and Montigny confirmed this by the accounts they sent home from Madrid of the alteration in the manner with which they were treated by Philip and his courtiers; and the Prince of Orange was more firmly decided in his. opinions of the coming vengeance of the tyrant.

William summoned his brother Louis, the Counts Egmont, Horn, and Hoogstraeten, to a secret conference at Termonde; and he there, submitted to them this letter of Alava's, with others which he had received from Spain, confirmatory of his worst fears. Louis of Nassau voted for open and instant rebellion: William recommended a cautious observance of the projects of government, not doubting but a fair pretext would be soon given to justify the most vigourous overt acts of revolt: but Egmont at once struck a death-blow to the energetic project of one brother, and the cautious amendment of the other, by declaring his present resolution to devote himself wholly to the service of the king, and on no inducement whatever to risk the perils of rebellion. He expressed his perfect reliance on the justice and the goodness of Philip, when once he should see the determined loyalty of those whom he had hitherto had so much reason to suspect; and he exhorted the others to follow his example.

The two brothers, and Count Horn implored him in their turn to abandon this blind reliance on the tyrant; but in vain. His new and unlooked for profession of faith completely paralyzed their plans. He possessed too largely the confidence of both the soldiery and the people, to make it possible to attempt any serious measure of resistance in which he would not take a part. The meeting broke up without coming to any decision. All those who bore a part in it were expected at Brussels to attend the council of state; Egmont alone repaired thither. The *governant* questioned him on the object of the conference at Termonde: he only replied by an indignant glance, at the same time presenting a copy of Alava's letter.

The *governant* now applied her whole efforts to destroy the union among the patriot lords. She, in the meantime, ordered levies of troops to the amount of some thousands, the command of which was given to the nobles on whose attachment she could reckon. The most vigourous measures were adopted. Noircarmes, Governor of Hainault, appeared before Valenciennes, which, being in the power of the Calvinists, had assumed a most determined attitude of resistance. He vainly summoned the place to submission, and to admit a royalist garrison; and on receiving an obstinate refusal, he commenced the siege in form. An undisciplined rabble of between 3000 and 4000 *gueux*, under the direction of John de Soreas, gathered together in the neighbourhood of Lille and Tournai, with a show of attacking these places. But the governor of the former town dispersed one party of them; and Noircarmes surprised and almost destroyed the main body—their leader falling in the action. (Bentivoglio.)

These were the first encounters of the civil war, which raged without cessation for upwards of forty years in these devoted countries, and which is universally allowed to be the most remarkable that ever desolated any isolated portion of Europe. The space which we have already given to the causes which produced this memorable revolution, now actually commenced, will not allow us to do more than rapidly sketch the fierce events that succeeded each other with frightful rapidity.

While Valenciennes prepared for a vigourous resistance, a general synod of the Protestants was held at Antwerp, and De Brederode undertook an attempt to see the *governant,* and lay before her the complaints of this body: but she refused to admit him into the capital. He then addressed to her a remonstrance in writing, in which he reproached her with her violation of the treaties, on the faith of which the confederates had dispersed, and the majority of the Protestants laid down their arms. He implored her to revoke the new proclamations, by which she prohibited them from the free exercise of their religion; and above all things, he insisted on the abandonment of the siege of Valenciennes, and the disbanding of the new levies. The *governant's* reply was one of haughty reproach and defiance. The gauntlet was now thrown down; no possible hope of reconciliation remained; and the whole country flew to arms. A sudden attempt on the part of the royalists, under Count Meghem, against Bois-le-duc, was repulsed by 800 men, commanded by an officer named Bomberg, in the immediate service of De Brederode, who had fortified himself in his garrison town of Vienen.

The Prince of Orange maintained at Antwerp an attitude of

extreme firmness and caution. His time for action had not yet arrived; but his advice and protection were of infinite importance on many occasions. John de Marnix, Lord of Toulouse, brother of Philip de St. Aldegonde, took possession of Osterweel on the Scheldt, a quarter of a league from Antwerp, and fortified himself in a strong position. But he was impetuously attacked by the Count de Lannoy with a considerable force, and perished, after a desperate defence, with full 1000 of his followers. Three hundred who laid down their arms, were immediately after the action butchered in cold blood. (Vandervynct.)

Antwerp was on this occasion saved from the excesses of its divided and furious citizens, and preserved from the horrors of pillage, by the calmness and intrepidity of the Prince of Orange. Valenciennes at length capitulated to the royalists, disheartened by the defeat and death of De Marnix, and terrified by a bombardment of thirty-six hours. The governor, two preachers, and about forty of the citizens, were hanged by the victors, and the reformed religion prohibited, Noircarmes promptly followed up his success. Maestricht, Turnhout, and Bois-le-duc submitted at his approach; and the insurgents were soon driven from all the provinces, Holland alone excepted. Brederode fled to Germany, where he died the following year. (Bentivoglio.)

The *governant* showed, in her success, no small proofs of decision. She and her counsellors, acting under orders from the king, were resolved on embarrassing to the utmost the patriot lords; and a new oath of allegiance, to be proposed to every functionary of the state, was considered as a certain means for attaining this object without the violence of an unmerited dismissal. The terms of this oath were strongly opposed to every principle of patriotism and toleration. Count Mansfield was the first of the nobles who took it. The Duke of Arschot, Counts Meghem, Berlaimont, and Egmont, followed his example. The Counts of Horn, Hoogstraeten, De Brederode, and others, refused on various pretexts. Every artifice and persuasion was tried to induce the Prince of Orange to subscribe to this new test; but his resolution had been for some time formed. He saw that every chance of constitutional resistance to tyranny was for the present at an end.

The time for petitioning was gone by. The confederation was dissolved. A royalist army was in the field; the Duke of Alva was notoriously approaching at the head of another, more numerous. It was worse than. useless to conclude a hollow convention with the *governant*, of mock loyalty on his part and mock confidence on hers.

Many other important considerations convinced William that his only honourable, safe, and wise course was to exile himself from the Netherlands altogether, until more propitious circumstances allowed of his acting openly, boldly, and with effect.

Before he put this plan of voluntary banishment into execution, he and Egmont had a parting interview, at the village of Willebroek, between Antwerp and Brussels. Count Mansfield, and Berti, secretary to the *governant*, were present at this memorable meeting. The details of what passed were reported to the confederates by one of their party, who contrived to conceal himself in the chimney of the chamber. (Schiller.) Nothing could exceed the energetic warmth with which the two illustrious friends reciprocally endeavoured to turn each other from their respective line of conduct; but in vain. Egmont's fatal confidence in the king was not to be shaken; nor was Nassau's penetrating mind to be deceived by the romantic delusion which led away his friend. They separated with most affectionate expressions; and Nassau was even moved to tears. His parting words were to the following effect:

> Confide, then, since it must be so, in the gratitude of the king; but a painful presentiment (God grant it may prove a false one!) tells me that you will serve the Spaniards as the bridge by which they will enter the country, and which they will destroy as soon as they have passed over it! (Vandervynct.)

On the 11th of April, a few days after this conference, the Prince of Orange set out for Germany, with his three brothers and his whole family, with the exception of his eldest son Philip William count de Beuren, whom he left behind a student in the university of Louvain. He believed that the privileges of the college and the franchises of Brabant would prove a sufficient protection to the youth; and this appears the only instance in which William's vigilant prudence was deceived. (Schiller.) The departure of the prince seemed to remove all hope of protection or support from the unfortunate Protestants, now left the prey of their implacable tyrant. The confederation of the nobles was completely broken up. The counts of Hoogstraeten, Bergen, and Culembourg, followed the example of the Prince of Orange, and escaped to Germany; and the greater number of those who remained behind took the new oath of allegiance, and became reconciled to the government. (Schiller.)

This total dispersion of the confederacy brought all the towns of Holland into obedience to the king. But the emigration which immediately commenced threatened the country with ruin. England and Germany swarmed with Dutch and Belgian refugees; and all the efforts of the *governant* could not restrain the thousands that took to flight. She was not more successful in her attempts to influence the measures of the king. She implored him, in repeated letters, to abandon his design of sending a foreign army into the country, which she represented as being now quite reduced to submission and tranquillity. She added, that the mere report of this royal invasion (so to call it) had already deprived the Netherlands of many thousands of its best inhabitants; and that the appearance of the troops would change it into a desert. These arguments, meant to dissuade, were the very means, of encouraging Philip in his design. He conceived his project to be now ripe for the complete suppression of freedom; and Alva soon began his march.

On the 5th of May, 1567, this celebrated certain, whose reputation was so quickly destined to sink into the notoriety of an executioner, began his memorable march; and on the 22nd of August, he, with his two natural sons, and his veteran army consisting of about 15,000 men, arrived at the walls of Brussels. (Bentivoglio.) The discipline observed on this march was a terrible forewarning to the people of the Netherlands of the influence of the general and the obedience of the troops. They had little chance of resistance against such soldiers so commanded.

Several of the Belgian nobility went forward to meet Alva, to render him the accustomed honours, and endeavour thus early to gain his good graces. Among them was the infatuated Egmont, who made a present to Alva of two superb horses, which the latter received with a disdainful air of condescension, (Schiller); Alva's first care was the distribution of his troops—several thousands of whom were placed in Antwerp, Ghent, and other important towns, and the remainder reserved under his own immediate orders at Brussels. His approach was celebrated by universal terror; and his arrival was thoroughly humiliating to the Duchess of Parma. He immediately produced his commission as commander-in-chief, of the royal armies in the Netherlands; but he next showed her another, which confided to him powers infinitely more extended than any Marguerite herself had enjoyed, and which proved to her that the almost sovereign power over the country was virtually vested in him.

Alva first turned his attention to the seizure of those patriot lords whose pertinacious infatuation left them within his reach. He summoned a meeting of all the members of the council of state and the knights of the order of the Golden Fleece, to deliberate on matters of great importance. Counts Egmont and Horn attended, among many others; and at the conclusion of the council they were both arrested (some historians—Strada and Vandervynct—assert by the hands of Alva and his eldest son), as was also Van Straeten *burgomaster* of Antwerp, and Casambrot, Egmont's secretary. The young Count of Mansfield appeared for a moment at this meeting; but, warned by his father of the fate intended him, as an original member of the confederation, he had time to fly. The Count of Hoogstraeten was happily detained by illness, and thus escaped the fate of his friends. Egmont and Horn were transferred to the citadel of Ghent, under, an escort of 3000 Spanish soldiers. Several other persons of the first families were arrested; and those who had originally been taken in arms were executed without delay. (Schiller.)

The next measures, of the new governor were the re-establishment of the inquisition, the promulgation of the decrees of the council of Trent, the revocation of the Duchess of Parma's edicts, and the royal refusal to recognise the terms of her treaties with the Protestants. He immediately established a special tribunal, composed of twelve members, with full powers to inquire into and pronounce judgment on every circumstance connected with the late troubles. He named himself president of this council, and appointed a Spaniard, named Vargas, as vice-president—a wretch of the most diabolical cruelty.

Several others of the judges were also Spaniards, in direct infraction of the fundamental laws of the country. This council, immortalized by its infamy, was named by the new governor (for so Alva was in fact, though not yet in name,) the Council of Troubles. By the people it was soon designed the Council of Blood. In its atrocious proceedings no respect was paid to titles, contracts, or privileges, however sacred. Its judgments were without appeal. Every subject of the state was amenable to its summons; clergy and laity, the first individuals of the country, as well as the most wretched outcasts of society.

Its decrees were passed with disgusting rapidity and contempt of form. Contumacy was punished with exile and confiscation. Those who, strong in innocence, dared to brave a trial, were lost without resource. The accused were forced to its bar without previous warning. Many a wealthy citizen was dragged to trial four leagues' distance, tied to a horse's tail. The number of victims was appalling.

On one occasion, the town of Valenciennes alone saw fifty-five of its citizens fall by the hands of the executioner. Hanging, beheading, quartering, and burning, were the everyday spectacles. The enormous confiscations only added to the thirst for sold and blood by which Alva and his satellites were parched. History offers no example of parallel honours: for while party vengeance on other occasions has led to scenes of fury and terror, they arose, in this instance, from the vilest cupidity and the most cold-blooded cruelty. (Schiller.)

After three months of such atrocity, Alva, fatigued rather than satiated with butchery, resigned his hateful functions wholly into the hands of Vargas, who was chiefly aided by the members Delrio and Dela Tone, Even at this remote period we cannot repress the indication excited by the mention of those monsters, and it is impossible not to feel satisfaction in fixing upon their names the brand of historic execration. One of these wretches, called Hesselts, used at length to sleep during the mock trials of the already doomed victims; and as often as he was roused up by his colleagues, he used to cry out mechanically, "To the gibbet! to the gibbet!" so familiar was his tongue with the sounds of condemnation. (Schiller.)

The despair of the people may be imagined from the fact, that until the end of the year 1567 their only consolation was the prospect of the king's arrival! He never dreamt of coming. Even the delight of feasting in horrors like these could not conquer his indolence. The good Duchess of Parma—for so she was in comparison with her successor—was not long left to oppose the feeble barrier of her prayers between Alva and his victims. She demanded her dismissal from the nominal dignity, which was now but a title of disgrace. Philip granted it readily, accompanied by a hypocritical letter, a present of 90,000 crowns, and the promise of an annual pension of 20,000 more. She left Brussels in the month of April, 1508, (De Thou), raised to a high place in the esteem and gratitude or the people, less by any actual claims from her own conduct, than by its fortuitous contrast with the infamy of her successor. She retired to Italy, and died at Naples in the month of February, 1566. (Vandervynct.)

Ferdinand Alvarez de Toledo Duke of Alva was of a distinguished family in Spain, and even boasted of his descent from one of the Moorish monarchs who had reigned in the insignificant kingdom of Toledo. When he assumed the chief command in the Netherlands, he was sixty years of age; having grown old and obdurate in pride, ferocity, and avarice. His deeds must stand instead of a more detailed portrait, which, to be thoroughly striking, should be traced with a pen dipped in blood. He was a fierce and clever soldier, brought up in the school of Charles V., and trained to his profession in the wars of that monarch in Germany, and subsequently in that of Philip II. against France. (Vandervynct.) In addition to the horrors acted by the council of blood, Alva committed many deeds of collateral but minor tyranny: among others, he issued a decree forbidding, under severe penalties, any inhabitant of the country to marry without his express permission. His furious edicts against emigration were attempted to be enforced in vain. Elizabeth of England opened all the ports of her kingdom to the Flemish refugees, (Van Meteren), who carried with them those abundant stares of manufacturing knowledge which she wisely knew to be the elements of national wealth.

Alva soon summoned the Prince of Orange, his brothers, and all the confederate lords, to appear before the council and answer to the charge of high treason. The prince gave a prompt and contemptuous answer, denying the authority of Alva and his council, and acknowledging for his judges only the emperor, whose vassal he was, or the king of Spain in person, as president of the order of the Golden Fleece. The other lords made replies nearly similar. The trials of each were, therefore, proceeded on, by contumacy; confiscation of property being an object almost as dear to the tyrant viceroy as the death of his victims. Judgments were promptly pronounced against those present or absent, alive or dead. Witness the case of the unfortunate Marquess of Bergues, who had previously expired at Madrid, as was universally believed, by poison; and his equally ill-fated colleague in the embassy, the Baron Montigny, was for a while imprisoned at Segovia, where he was soon after secretly beheaded, on the base pretext of former disaffection. (Vandervynct.)

The departure of the Duchess of Parma having left Alva undisputed as well as unlimited authority, he proceeded rapidly in his terrible career. The Count of Beuren was seized at Louvain, and sent prisoner to Madrid; and wherever it was possible to lay hands on a suspected patriot, the occasion was not neglected. It would be a revolting task to enter into a minute detail of all the horrors committed, and impossible to record the names of the victims who so quickly fell before Alva's insatiate cruelty. The people were driven to frenzy. Bands of wretches fled to the woods and marshes; whence, half famished and perishing for want, they revenged themselves with pillage and murder. Pirates infested and ravaged the coast; and thus, from both sea and land, the whole extent of the Netherlands was devoted to carnage and ruin. (Vandervynct.)

The chronicles of Brabant and Holland, (Batavia illustrated) chiefly written in Flemish by contemporary authors, abound in thrilling details of the horrors of this general desolation, with long lists of those who perished. Suffice it to say, that on the recorded boast of Alva himself, he caused 18,000 inhabitants of the Low Countries to perish by the hands of the executioner, during his less than six years' sovereignty in the Netherlands. (Grotius.)!

The most important of these tragical scenes was now soon to be acted. The Counts Egmont and Horn, having submitted to some previous interrogatories by Vargas and others, were removed from Ghent to Brussels, on the 3rd of June, under a strong escort. The following day they passed through the mockery of a trial before the council of blood; and on the 5th, they were both beheaded in the great square of Brussels, in the presence of Alva, who gloated on the spectacle from a balcony that commanded the execution. The same day Vanstraelen and Casambrot shared the fate of their illustrious friends, in the castle of Vilvorde; with many others, whose names only find a place in the local chronicles of the times. Egmont and Horn met their fate with the firmness expected from their well-proved courage.

These judicial murders excited in the Netherlands an agitation without bounds. It was no longer hatred or aversion that filled men's minds, but fury and despair. The out-bursting of a general revolt was hourly watched for. The foreign powers, without exception, expressed their disapproval of these executions. The emperor Maximilian II., and all the Catholic princes, condemned them. The former sent his brother expressly to the King of Spain, to warn him, that without a cessation of his cruelties, he could not restrain a general declaration from the members of the empire, which would, in all likelihood, deprive him of every acre of land in the Netherlands. (Vandervynct.) The princes of the Protestant states held no terms in the expression of their disgust and resentment; and everything seemed now ripe, both at home and abroad, to favour the enterprise on which the Prince of Orange was determined to risk his fortune and his life.

But his principal resources were to be found in his genius and courage, and in the heroic devotion partaken by his whole family in the cause of their country. His brother, Count John, advanced him a considerable sum of money; the Flemings and Hollanders, in England and elsewhere, subscribed largely; the prince himself after raising loans in every possible way on his private means, sold his jewels, his plate, and even the furniture of his houses, and threw the amount into the common fund.

Two remarkable events took place this year in Spain, and added to the general odium entertained against Philip's character throughout Europe. The first was the death of his son don Carlos, whose sad story is too well known in connexion with the annals of his country to require a place here; the other was the death of the queen. Universal opinion assigned poison as the cause (Vandervynct); and Charles IX. of France, her brother, who loved her with great tenderness, seems to have joined in this belief. Astonishment and horror filled all minds on the double denouement of this romantic tragedy; and the enemies of the tyrant reaped all the advantages it was so well adapted to produce them.

The Prince of Orange, having raised a considerable force in Germany, now entered on the war with all the well-directed energy by which he was characterized. The Queen of England, the French Huguenots, and the Protestant princes of Germany, all lent him their aid in money, or in men; and he opened his first campaign with great advantage. He formed his army into four several corps, intending to enter the country on as many different points, and by a sudden irruption on that most vulnerable to rouse at once the hopes and the co-operation of the people. His brothers Louis and Adolphus, at the head of one of these divisions, penetrated into Friesland, and there commenced the contest.

The Count of Aremberg, governor of this province, assisted by the Spanish troops. under Gonsalvo de Bracamonte, quickly opposed the invaders. They met on the 24th of May near the abbey of Heiligerlee, which gave its name to the battle; and after a short contest the royalists were defeated with great loss. The Count of Aremberg and Adolphus of Nassau encountered in single combat, and fell by each other's hands. (Strada.) The victory was dearly purchased by the loss of this gallant prince, the first of his illustrious family, who have on so many occasions, down to these very days, freely shed their blood for the freedom and happiness of the country which may be so emphatically called their own.

Alva immediately hastened to the scene of this first action, and soon forced Count Louis to another at a place called Jemminghem, near the town of Embden, on the 21st of July. Their forces were nearly equal, about 14,000 on either side; but all the advantage of discipline and skill was in favour of Alva; and the consequence was, the total rout of the patriots with a considerable loss in killed and the whole of the cannon and baggage. The entire province of Friesland was thus again reduced to obedience, and Alva hastened back to Brabant to make head against the Prince of Orange. The latter had now under his command an army of 28,000 men—an imposing force in point of numbers, being double that which his rival was able to muster. He soon made himself master of the towns of Tongres and St. Trond, and the whole province of Liege was in his power.

He advanced boldly against Alva, and for several months did all that manoeuvring could do to force him to a battle. But the wily veteran knew his trade too well; he felt sure that in time the prince's force would disperse for want of pay and supplies; and he managed his resources so ably, that with little risk and scarcely any loss he finally succeeded in his object. In the month of October, the prince found himself forced to disband his large but undisciplined force; and he retired into France to recruit his funds and consider on the best measures for some future enterprise.

The insolent triumph of Alva knew no bounds. The rest of the year was consumed in new executions. The hotel of Culembourg, the early cradle of De Brederode's confederacy, was rased to the ground, and a pillar erected on the spot commemorative of the deed; while Alva, resolved to erect a monument of his success as well as of his hate, had his own statue in brass, formed of the cannons taken at Jemminghem, set up in the citadel of Antwerp, with various symbols of power and an inscription of inflated pride.

The following year was ushered in by a demand of unwonted and extravagant rapacity; the establishment of two taxes on property, personal and real, to the amount of the hundredth penny (or *denier*) on each kind; and at every transfer or sale, ten *per cent* on personal, and five *per cent* for real property. The stated-general, of whom this demand was made, were unanimous in their opposition, as well as the ministers; but particularly De Berlaimont and Viglius. Alva was so irritated that he even menaced the venerable president of the council, but could not succeed in intimidating him. He obstinately persisted in his design for a considerable period; resisting arguments and prayers, and even the more likely means tried for softening his cupidity, by furnishing him with sums from other sources equivalent to those which the new taxes were calculated to produce. (Vandervynct.) To his repeated threats against Viglius the latter replied, that:

He was convinced the king would not condemn him unheard; but that at any rate his grey hairs saved him from any ignoble fear of death. (Viglii Comment.)

A deputation was sent from the states-general to Philip, explaining the impossibility of persevering in the attempted taxes, which were incompatible with every principle of commercial liberty. (De Neny, *Mém. Hist, et Pol. sur les Pays Bas*.) But Alva would not abandon his design till he had forced every province into resistance, and the king himself commanded him to desist. The events of this and the following year (1570) may be shortly summed up; none of any striking interest or eventual importance having occurred. The sufferings of the country were increasing from day to day under the intolerable tyranny which bore it down. The patriots attempted nothing on land; but their naval force began from this time to acquire that consistency and power which was so soon to render it the chief means of resistance and the great source of wealth.

The privateers or *corsairs*, which began to swarm from every port in Holland and Zealand, and which found refuge in all those of England, sullied many gallant exploits by instances of culpable excess; so much so, that the Prince of Orange was forced to withdraw the command which he had delegated to the Lord of Dolhain, and to replace him by Gislain de Fiennes: for already several of the exiled nobles and ruined merchants of Antwerp and Amsterdam had joined these bold adventurers; and purchased or built, with the remnant of their fortunes, many vessels, in which they carried on a most productive warfare against Spanish commerce through the whole extent of the English Channel, from the mouth of the Embs to the harbour of La Rochelle. (Vandervynct.)

One of those frightful inundations to which the northern provinces were so constantly exposed, occurred this year, carrying away the dikes, and destroying lives and property to a considerable amount. In Friesland alone 20,000 men were victims to this calamity. But no suffering could affect the inflexible sternness of the Duke of Alva; and to such excess did he carry his persecution, that Philip himself began to be discontented, and thought his representative was overstepping the bounds of delegated tyranny. He even reproached him sharply in some of his dispatches. The governor replied in the same strain; and such was the effect of this correspondence, that Philip resolved to remove him from his command.

But the king's marriage with Anne of Austria, daughter of the Emperor Maximilian, obliged him to defer his intentions for a while; and he at length named John de la Cerda, Duke of Medina-Celi, for Alva's successor. Upwards of a year, however, elapsed before this new governor was finally appointed; and he made his appearance on the coast of Flanders with a considerable fleet, on the 11th of May, 1572. He was afforded on this very day a specimen of the sort of people he came to contend with; for his fleet was suddenly attacked by that of the patriots, and many of his vessels burned and taken before his eyes, with their rich cargoes and considerable treasures intended for the service of the state. (Vandervynct.)

The Duke of Medina-Celi proceeded rapidly to Brussels, where he was ceremoniously received by Alva, who however refused to resign the government, under the pretext that the term of his appointment had not expired, and that he was resolved first to completely suppress all symptoms of revolt in the northern provinces. He succeeded in effectually disgusting La Cerda, who almost immediately demanded and obtained his own recall to Spain. Alva, left once more in undisputed possession of his power, turned it with increased vigour into new channels of oppression.

He was soon again employed in efforts to effect the levying of his favourite taxes; and such was the resolution of the tradesmen of Brussels, that, sooner than submit, they almost universally closed their shops altogether. Alva, furious at this measure, caused sixty of the citizens to be seized, and ordered them to be hanged opposite their own doors. The gibbets were actually erected, when, on the very morning of the day fixed for the executions, he received dispatches that wholly disconcerted him, and stopped their completion. (Vandervynct.)

To avoid an open rupture with Spain, the Queen of England had just at this time interdicted the Dutch and Flemish privateers from taking shelter in her ports. William de la Marck Count of Lunoy had now the chief command of this adventurous force. He was distinguished by an inveterate hatred against the Spaniards, and had made a wild and romantic vow never to cut his hair or beard till he had avenged the murders of Egmont and Horn. He was impetuous and terrible in all his actions, and bore the surname of "the wild boar of the Ardennes." Driven out of the harbours of England, he resolved on some desperate enterprise; and on the 1st of April he succeeded in surprising the little town of Brille, in the island of Voorn, situate between Zealand and Holland, This insignificant place acquired great celebrity from this event, which may be considered the first successful step towards the establishment of liberty and the republic. (Vandervynct.)

Alva was confounded by the news of this exploit, but with his usual activity he immediately turned his whole attention towards the point of greatest danger. His embarrassment, however, became every day more considerable. Lunoy's success was the signal of a general revolt. In a few days every town in Holland and Zealand declared for liberty, with the exception of Amsterdam and Middleburg, where the Spanish garrisons were too strong for the people to attempt their expulsion.

The Prince of Orange, who had been on the watch for a favourable moment, now entered Brabant at the head of 20,000 men, composed of French, German, and English, and made himself master of several important places; while his indefatigable brother Louis, with a minor force, suddenly appeared in Hainault, and, joined by a large body of French Huguenots under De Genlis, he seized on Mons, the capital of the province, on the 25th of May.

Alva turned first towards the recovery of this important place, and gave the command of the siege to his son Frederic of Toledo, who was assisted by the counsels of Noircarmes and Vitelli; but Louis of Nassau held out for upwards of three months, and only surrendered on an honourable capitulation in the month of September; his French allies having been first entirely defeated, and their brave leader De Genlis taken prisoner. The Prince of Orange had in the meantime secured possession of Louvaine, Ruremonde, Mechlin, and other towns, carried Termonde and Oudenarde by assault, and made demonstrations which seemed, to court Alva once more to try the fortune of the campaign in a pitched battle.

But such were not William's real intentions, (Vandervynct) nor did the cautious tactics of his able opponent allow him to provoke such a risk. He, however, ordered his son Frederic to march with all his force into Holland, and he soon undertook the siege of Haerlem. By the time that Mons fell again into the power of the Spaniards, sixty-five towns and their territories, chiefly in the northern provinces, had thrown off the yoke. The single port of Flessingue contained 150 patriot vessels, well armed and equipped, (Cerisier); and from that epoch may be dated the rapid growth of the first naval power in Europe, with the single exception of Great Britain.

It is here worthy of remark, that all the horrors of which the people of Flanders were the victims, and in their full proportion, had not the effect of exciting them to revolt; but they rose up with fury against the payment of the new taxes. They sacrificed everything sooner than pay these unjust exactions—*Omnia dabant, ne decimam darant.* (Grotius.) The next important event in these wars was the siege of Haerlem, before which place the Spaniards were arrested in their progress for seven months, and which they at length succeeded in taking with a loss of 10,000 men.

The details of this memorable siege are calculated to arouse every feeling of pity for the heroic defenders, and of execration against the cruel assailants. A widow, named Kenau Hasselaer, gained a niche in history by her remarkable valour at the head of a battalion of 300 of her townswomen, who bore a part in all the labours and perils of the siege. (Strada.) After the surrender, and in pursuance of Alva's common system, his ferocious son caused the governor and the other chief officers to be beheaded; and upwards of 2000 of the worn-out garrison and *burghers* were either put to the sword, or tied two and two, and drowned in the lake which gives its name to the town. (Bentivoglio.)

Tergoes in South Beveland, Mechlin, Naerden, and other towns, were about the same period the scenes of gallant actions, and of subsequent cruelties of the most revolting nature as soon as they fell into the power of the Spaniards.

******

Strada, with all his bigotry to the Spanish cause, admits that these excesses were atrocious crimes rather than just punishments: *non paena, sed flagitium.*

******

Horrors like these were sure to force reprisals on the part of the maddened patriots. De la Marck carried on his daring exploits with a cruelty which excited the indignation of the Prince of Orange, by whom he was removed from his command. The contest was for a while prosecuted, with a decrease of vigour proportioned to the serious losses on both sides; money and the munitions of war began to fail; and though the Spaniards succeeded in taking The Hague, they were repulsed before Alkmaer with great loss, and their fleet was almost entirely destroyed in a naval combat on the Zuyder Zee. The Count Bossu, their admiral, was taken in this fight, with about 900 of his best sailors.

Holland was now from one end to the other the theatre of the most shocking events. While the people performed deeds of the greatest heroism, the perfidy and cruelty of the Spaniards had no bounds. The patriots saw more danger in submission than in resistance; each town, which was in succession subdued, endured the last extremities of suffering before it yielded, and victory was frequently the consequence of despair. (Grotius, Strada and Bentivoglio.) This unlooked-for turn in affairs decided the king to remove Alva, whose barbarous and rapacious conduct was now objected to even by Philip, when it produced results disastrous to his cause. Don Luis Zanega y Requesens, commander of the order of Malta, was named to the government of the Netherlands. He arrived at Brussels on the 17th of November, 1573; and on the 18th of the following month, the monster whom he succeeded set out for Spain, loaded with the booty to which he had waded through oceans of blood, and with the curses of the country, which, however, owed its subsequent freedom to the impulse given by his intolerable cruelty. He repaired to Spain; and after various fluctuations of favour and disgrace at the hands of his congenial master, he died in his bed, at Lisbon, in 1582, at the advanced age of seventy-four years.

CHAPTER 4

1573–1576

TO THE PACIFICATION OF GHENT.

The character of Requesens was not more opposed to that of his predecessor, than were the instructions given to him for his government. He was an honest, well-meaning, and moderate man, (De Thou) and the king of Spain hoped, that by his influence and a total change of measures, he might succeed in recalling the Netherlands to obedience. But, happily for the country, this change was adopted too late for success; and the weakness of the new government completed the glorious results, which the ferocity of the former had prepared.

Requesens performed all that depended on him, to gain the confidence of the people. He caused Alva's statue to be removed; and hoped to efface the memory of the tyrant, by dissolving the council of blood, and abandoning the obnoxious taxes which their inventor had suspended rather than abolished. A general amnesty was also promulgated against the revolted provinces: they received it with contempt and defiance. Nothing then was left to Requesens but to renew the war; and this he found to be a matter of no easy execution. The finances were in a state of the greatest confusion; and the Spanish troops were in many places seditious, in some openly mutinous, Alva having left large arrears of pay due to almost all, notwithstanding the immense amount of his pillage and extortion. (Vandervynct.)

Middleburg, which had long sustained a siege against all the efforts of the patriots, was now nearly reduced by famine, notwithstanding the gallant efforts of its governor, Mondragon. Requesens turned his immediate attention to the relief of this important place; and he soon assembled, at Antwerp and Bergen-op-Zoom, a fleet of sixty vessels for that purpose. But Louis Boisot, admiral of Zealand, promptly repaired to attack this force; and after a severe action he totally defeated it, and killed De Glimes, one of its admirals, under the eyes of Requesens himself, who, accompanied by his suite, stood during the whole affair on the dike of Schakerloo. (Vandervynct.) This action took place the 29th of January, 1574; and, on the 19th of February following, Middleburg surrendered, after a resistance of two years. The Prince of Orange granted such conditions as were due to the bravery of the governor; and thus, set an example of generosity and honour which greatly changed the complexion of the war. (Meteren.)

All Zealand was now free; and the intrepid admiral Boisot gained another victory on the 30th of May—destroying several of the Spanish vessels, and taking some others, with their admiral Von Haemstede. Frequent naval enterprises were also undertaken against the frontiers of Flanders; and while the naval forces thus harassed the enemy on every vulnerable point, the unfortunate provinces of the interior were ravaged by the mutinous and revolted Spaniards, and by the native brigands, who pillaged both royalists and patriots with atrocious impartiality.

To these manifold evils was now added one more terrible, in the appearance of the plague, which broke out at Ghent in the month of October, and devastated a peat part of the Netherlands; not, however, with that violence with which it rages in more southern climates. (Vandervynct.)

Requesens, overwhelmed by difficulties, yet exerted himself to the utmost to put the best face on the affairs of government. His chief care was to appease the mutinous soldiery: he even caused his plate to be melted, and freely gave the produce towards the payment of their arrears. The patriots, well informed of this state of things, laboured to turn it to their best advantage. They opened the campaign in the province of Guelders, where Louis of Nassau, with his younger brother Henry, and the prince Palatine, son of the elector Frederick III., appeared at the head of 11,000 men: The Prince of Orange prepared to join him with an equal number; but Requesens promptly dispatched Sanchez d'Avila to prevent this junction. The Spanish commander quickly passed the Meuse near Nimeguen; and on the 14th of April he forced Count Louis to a battle, on the great plain called Mookerheyde, close to the village of Mook.

The royalists attacked with their usual valour; and after two hours of hard fighting, the confederates were totally defeated. The three gallant princes were among the slain, and their bodies were never afterwards discovered. It has been stated, on doubtful authority, that Louis of Nassau, after having lain some time among the heaps of dead, dragged himself to the side of the River Meuse, and while washing his wounds, was inhumanly murdered by some straggling peasants, to whom he was unknown. (Haræus.) The unfortunate fate of this enterprising prince was a severe blow to the patriot cause, and a cruel affliction to the Prince of Orange. He had now already lost three brothers in the war; and remained alone, to revenge their fate, and sustain the cause for which they had perished.

D'Avila soon found his victory to be as fruitless as it was brilliant. The ruffian troops, by whom it was gained, became immediately self-disbanded; threw off all authority; hastened to possess themselves of Antwerp; and threatened to proceed to the most horrible extremities, if their pay was longer withheld. The citizens succeeded with difficulty in appeasing them, by the sacrifice of some money in part payment of their claims. Requesens took advantage of their temporary calm, and dispatched them promptly to take part in the siege of Leyden. (Vandervynct.)

This siege formed another of those numerous instances which became so memorable from the mixture of heroism and horror. Jean Vanderdoes, known in literature by the name of Dousa, and celebrated for his Latin poems, commanded the place. Valdez, who conducted the siege, urged Dousa to surrender; when the latter replied, in the name of the inhabitants, that:

When provisions failed them, they would devour their left hands, reserving the right to defend their liberty.

A party of the inhabitants, driven to disobedience and revolt by the excess of misery to which they were shortly reduced, attempted to force the *burgomaster*, Vanderwerf, to supply them with bread, or yield up the place. But he sternly made the celebrated answer, which cannot be remembered without shuddering—

Bread I have none; but if my death can afford you relief tear my body in pieces, and let those who are most hungry devour it!

But in this extremity relief at last was afforded by the decisive measures of the Prince of Orange, who ordered all the neighbouring dikes to be opened and the sluices raised, thus sweeping away the besiegers on the waves of the ocean: the inhabitants of Leyden were apprised of this intention by means of letters intrusted to the safe carriage of pigeons trained for the purpose. (Strada.) The inundation was no sooner effected, than hundreds of flat-bottomed boats brought abundance of supplies to the half-famished town; while a violent storm carried the sea across the country for twenty leagues around, and destroyed the Spanish camp, with above 1000 soldiers, who were overtaken by the flood. This deliverance took place on the 3rd of October, on which day it is still annually celebrated by the descendants of the grateful citizens. (Vandervynct.)

It was now for the first time that Spain would consent to listen to advice or mediation, which had for its object the termination of this frightful war. The emperor Maximilian II. renewed at this epoch his efforts with Philip; and under such favourable auspices conferences commenced at Breda, where the Counts Swartzenberg and Hohenloe, brothers-in-law of the Prince of Orange, met, on the part of the emperor, the deputies from the King of Spain and the patriots; and hopes of a complete pacification were generally entertained. But three months of deliberation proved their fallacy. The patriots demanded toleration for the reformed religion. The king's deputies obstinately refused it. The congress was therefore broken up; and both oppressors and oppressed resumed their arms with increased vigour and tenfold desperation.

Requesens had long fixed his eyes on Zealand as the scene of an expedition by which he hoped to repair the failure before Leyden; and he caused an attempt, to be made on the town of Zuriczee, in the island of Scauwen, which merits record as one of the boldest and most original enterprises of the war.

The little islands of Zealand are separated from each other by narrow branches of the sea, which are fordable at low water; and it was by such a passage, two leagues in breadth, and till then untried, that the Spanish detachment of 1750 men, under Ulloa and other veteran captains, advanced to their exploit in the midst of dangers greatly increased by a night of total darkness. Each man carried round his neck two pounds of gunpowder, with a sufficient supply of biscuit for two days; and holding their swords and muskets high over their heads, they boldly waded forward, three abreast, in some places up to their shoulders in water.

The alarm was soon given, and a shower of balls was poured upon the gallant band, from upwards of forty boats which the Zealanders sent rapidly towards the spot. The only light afforded to either party was from the flashes of their guns; and while the adventurers advanced with undaunted firmness, their equally daring assailants, jumping from their boats into the water, attacked them with oars and hooked handspikes, by which many of the Spaniards were destroyed. The rear-guard, in this extremity, cut off from their companions, was obliged to retreat; but the rest, after a considerable loss, at length reached the land, and thus gained possession of the island, on the night of the 28th of September, 1575. (Strada.)

Requesens quickly afterwards repaired to the scene of this gallant exploit, and commenced the siege of Zuriczee, which he did not live to see completed. After having passed the winter months in preparations for the success of this object which he had so much at heart, he was recalled to Brussels by accounts of new mutinies in the Spanish cavalry; and the very evening before he reached the city he was attacked by a violent fever, which carried him off five days afterwards, on the 5th of March, 1576. (Bentivoglio.)

The suddenness of Requesen's illness had not allowed time for even the nomination of a successor, to which he was authorised by letters patent from the king. It is believed that his intention was to appoint Count Mansfield to the command of the army, and De Berlaiment to the administration of civil affairs. (Strada.) The government, however, now devolved entirely into the hands of the council of state, which was at that period composed of nine members. The principal of these was Philip de Croi Duke of Arschot; the other leading members were Viglius, Counts Mansfield and Berlaimont; and the council was degraded by numbering, among the rest, Debris and De Roda, two of the notorious Spaniards who had formed part of the council of blood.

The long resolved to leave the authority in the hands of this incongruous mixture, until the arrival of Don John of Austria, his natural brother, whom he had already named to the office of governor-general. But in the interval the government assumed an aspect of unprecedented disorder; and widespread anarchy embraced the whole country. The royal troops openly revolted, and fought against each other like deadly enemies. The nobles, divided in their views, arrogated to themselves in different places the titles and powers of command. Public faith and private probity seemed alike destroyed. Pillage, violence, and ferocity, were the commonplace characteristics of the times. (Bentivoglio.)

Circumstances like these may be well supposed to have revived the hopes of the Prince of Orange, who quickly saw amidst this chaos the elements of order, strength, and liberty. Such had been his previous affliction at the harrowing events which he witnessed, and despaired of being able to relieve, that he had proposed to the patriots of Holland and Zealand to destroy the dikes, submerge the whole country, and abandon to the waves the soil which refused security to freedom. But Providence destined him to be the saviour, instead of the destroyer, of his country. The chief motive of this excessive desperation had been the apparent desertion by Queen Elizabeth of the cause which she had hitherto so mainly assisted. Offended at the capture of some English ships by the Dutch, who asserted that they carried supplies for the Spaniards, she withdrew from them her protection: but by timely submission they appeased her wrath; and it is thought by some historians, that even thus early the Prince of Orange proposed to place the revolted provinces wholly under her protection. This, however, she for the time refused; but she strongly solicited Philip's mercy for these unfortunate countries, through the Spanish ambassador at her court.

In the meantime, the council of state at Brussels seemed disposed to follow up as for as possible the plans of Requesens. The siege of Zuriczee was continued; but speedy dissensions among the members of the government rendered their authority contemptible, if not utterly extinct, in the eyes of the people. The exhaustion of the treasury deprived them of all power to put an end to the mutinous excesses of the Spanish troops, and the latter carried their licentiousness to the utmost bounds. Zuriczee, admitted to a surrender, and saved from pillage by the payment of a large sum, was lost to the royalists within three months, from the want of discipline in its garrison; and the towns and *burghs* of Brabant suffered as much from the excesses of their nominal protectors as could have been inflicted by the enemy.

The mutineers at length, to the number of some thousands, attacked and carried by force the town of Alost, at equal distances between Brussels, Ghent, and Antwerp; imprisoned the chief citizens; and levied contributions on all the country round. It was then that the council of state found itself forced to proclaim them rebels, traitors, and enemies to the king and the country, and called on all loyal subjects to pursue and exterminate them wherever they were found in arms. (Bentivoglio.)

This proscription of the Spanish mutineers was followed by the convocation of the states–general; and the government thus hoped to maintain some show of union, and some chance of authority. But a new scene of intestine violence completed the picture of executive inefficiency. On the 4th of September, the grand bailiff of Brabant, as lieutenant of the Baron de Hesse, governor of Brussels, entered the council-chamber by force, and arrested all the members present, on suspicion of treacherously maintaining intelligence with the Spaniards. Counts Mansfield and Berlaimont were imprisoned, with some others. Viglius escaped this indignity by being absent from indisposition. This bold measure was hailed by the people with unusual joy, as the signal for that total change in the government which they reckoned on as the prelude to complete freedom.

The states-general were all at this time assembled, with the exception of those of Flanders, who joined the others with but little delay. The general reprobation against the Spaniards procured a second decree of proscription; and their desperate conduct justified the utmost violence with which they might be pursued. They still held the citadels of Ghent and Antwerp, as well as Maestricht, which they had seized on, sacked, and pillaged with all the fury which a barbarous enemy inflicts on a town carried by assault. On the 3rd of November, the other body of mutineers, in possession of Alost, marched to the support of their fellow brigands in the citadel of Antwerp; and both, simultaneously attacking this magnificent city, became masters of it in all points, in spite of a vigorous resistance on the part of the citizens.

They then began a scene of rapine and destruction unequalled in the annals of these desperate wars. More than 500 private mansions and the splendid town-house were delivered to the flames: 7000 citizens perished by the sword or in the waters of the Scheldt. For three days the carnage and the pillage went on with unheard-of fury; and the most opulent town in Europe was thus reduced to ruin and desolation by a few thousand frantic ruffians. The loss was valued at above 2,000,000 golden crowns. Vargas and Romero were the principal leaders of this infernal exploit; and De Roda gained a new title to his immortality of shame, by standing forth as its apologist.

The states-general, assembled at Ghent, were solemnly opened on the 14th of September. Being apprehensive of a sudden attack from the Spanish troops in the citadel, they proposed a negotiation, and demanded a protecting force from the Prince of Orange, who immediately entered into a treaty with their envoy, and sent to their assistance eight companies of infantry and seventeen pieces of cannon, under the command of the English colonel Temple. (Vandervynct.) In the midst of this turmoil and apparent insecurity, the states-general proceeded in their great work, and assumed the reins of government in the name of the king. They allowed the council of state still nominally to exist, but they restricted its powers far within those it had hitherto exercised; and the government, thus absolutely assuming the form of a republic, issued manifestoes in justification of its conduct, and demanded succour from all the foreign powers. To complete the union between the various provinces, it was resolved to resume the negotiations commenced the preceding year at Breda; and the 10th of October was fixed for this new congress to be held in the town-house of Ghent

On the day appointed, the congress opened its sittings; and rapidly arriving at the termination of its important object, the celebrated treaty known by the title of *The Pacification of Ghent* was published on the 8th of November, to the sound of bells and trumpets; while the ceremony was rendered still more imposing by the thunder of the artillery which battered the walls of the besieged citadel. It was even intended to have delivered a general assault against the place at the moment of the proclamation; but the mutineers demanded a capitulation, and finally surrendered three days afterwards. It was the wife of the famous Mondragon who commanded the place in her husband's absence; and by her heroism gave a new proof of the capability of the sex to surpass the limits which nature seems to have fixed for their conduct

The *Pacificatian* contained twenty-five articles:—amongst others, it was agreed:—

That a full amnesty should be passed for all offences whatsoever.

That the estates of Brabant, Flanders, Hainault, Artois, and others, on the one part; the Prince of Orange, and the states of Holland and Zealand and their associates, on the other; promised to maintain good faith, peace, and friendship, firm and inviolable; to mutually assist each other, at all times, in council and action; and to employ life and fortune, above all things, to expel from the country the Spanish soldiers and other foreigners.

That no one should be allowed to injure or insult, by word or deed, the exercise of the Catholic religion, on pain of being treated as a disturber of the public peace.

That the edicts against heresy and the proclamations of the Duke of Alva should be suspended.

That all confiscations, sentences, and judgments rendered since 1566, should be annulled.

That the inscriptions, monuments, and trophies erected by the Duke of Alva should be demolished.

Such were the general conditions of the treaty; the remaining articles chiefly concerned individual interests. The promulgation of this great charter of union, which was considered as the fundamental law of the country, was hailed in all parts of the Netherlands with extravagant demonstrations of joy.

CHAPTER 5

1576–1580

On the very day of the sack of Antwerp, Don John of Austria arrived at Luxembourg. This ominous commencement of his vice-regal reign was not belied by the events which followed; and the hero of Lepanto, the victor of the Turks, the idol of Christendom, was destined to have his reputation and well-won laurels tarnished in the service of the insidious despotism to which he now became an instrument. Don John was a natural son of Charles V., and to fine talents and a good disposition united the advantages of hereditary courage and a liberal education. He was born at Ratisbon, on the 24th of February, 1543. (Strada.)

His reputed mother was a young lady of that place, named Barbara Blomberg: but one historian states, that the real parent was of a condition too elevated to have her rank betrayed; and that, to conceal the mystery, Barbara Blomberg had voluntarily assumed the distinction, (Amelot de la Houssaye), or the dishonour, according to the different constructions put upon the case. The prince, having passed through France, disguised, for greater secrecy or in a youthful frolic, as a negro valet to Prince Octavo Gonzaga, (Strada), entered on the limits of his new government, and immediately wrote to the council of state in the most condescending terms to announce his arrival. (Bentivoglio.)

Nothing could present a less promising aspect to the prince than the country at the head of which he was now placed. He found all its provinces, with the sole exception of Luxembourg, in the anarchy attendant on a ten years' civil war, and apparently resolved on a total breach or their allegiance to Spain. He found his best, indeed his only, course to be that of moderation and management; and it is most probable that at the outset his intentions were really honourable and candid.

The states-general were not less embarrassed than the prince. His sudden arrival threw them into great perplexity, which was increased by the conciliatory tone of his letter. They had now removed from Ghent to Brussels; and first sending deputies to pay the honours of a ceremonious welcome to Don John, they wrote to the Prince of Orange, then in Holland, for his advice in this difficult conjuncture. The prince replied by a memorial of considerable length, dated Middleburg, the 30th of November, in which he gave them the most wise and prudent advice; the substance of which was to receive any propositions coming from the wily and perfidious Philip with the utmost suspicion, and to refuse all negotiation with his deputy, if the immediate withdrawal of the foreign troops was not at once conceded, and the acceptance of the pacification guarantied in its most ample extent. (Meteren.)

This advice was implicitly followed; the states in the meantime taking the precaution of assembling a large body of troops at Wavre, between Brussels and Namur, the command of which was given to the count of Lalain. A still more important measure was the dispatch of an envoy to England, to implore the assistance of Elizabeth. She acted on this occasion with frankness and intrepidity; giving a distinguished reception to the envoy De Sweveghem, and advancing a loan of 100,000*l*, sterling, on condition that the states made no treaty without her knowledge or participation. (Meteren.)

To secure still more closely the federal union that now bound the different provinces, a new compact was concluded by the deputies on the 9th of January, 1577, known by the title of *The Union of Brussels*, and signed by the prelates, ecclesiastics, lords, gentlemen, magistrates, and others, representing the estates of the Netherlands. A copy of this act of union was transmitted to Don John, to enable him thoroughly to understand the present state of feeling among those with whom he was now about to negotiate. He maintained a general tone of great moderation throughout the conference which immediately took place; and idler some months of cautious parleying, in the latter part of which the candour of the prince seemed doubtful, and which the native historians do not hesitate to stigmatise as merely assumed, a treaty was signed at Marche-en-Famenne, a place between Namur and Luxembourg, in which every point insisted on by the states was, to the surprise and delight of the nation, fully consented to and guarantied. This important document is called *The Perpetual Edict*, bears date the 12th of February, 1577, and contains nineteen articles. They were all based on the acceptance of the Pacification; but one expressly stipulated that the Count of Beuren should be set at liberty, as soon as the Prince of Orange, his father, had on his part ratified the treaty. (Vandervynct.)

Don John made his solemn entry into Brussels on the 1st of May, and assumed the functions of his limited authority. The conditions of the treaty were promptly and regularly fulfilled. The citadels occupied by the Spanish soldiers were given up to the Flemish and Walloon troops; and the departure of these ferocious foreigners took place at once. The large sums required to facilitate this measure made it necessary to submit for a while to the presence of the German mercenaries. But Don John's conduct soon destroyed the temporary delusion which had deceived the country.

Whether his projects were hitherto only concealed, or that they were now for the first time excited by the disappointment of those hopes of authority held out to him by Philip, and which his predecessors had shared, it is certain that he very early displayed his ambition, and very imprudently attempted to put it in force. He at once demanded from the council of state the command of the troops and the disposal of the revenues. The answer was a simple reference to the Pacification of Ghent; and the prince's rejoinder was an apparent submission, and the immediate dispatch of letters in cipher to the king, demanding a supply of troops sufficient to restore his ruined authority. These letters were intercepted by the King of Navarre, afterwards Henry IV. of Prance, who immediately transmitted them to the Prince of Orange, his old friend and fellow-soldier.

Public opinion, to the suspicions of which Don John had been from the first obnoxious, was now unanimous in attributing to design all that was unconstitutional and unfair. His impetuous character could no longer submit to the restraint of dissimulation, and he resolved to take some bold and decided measure. A very favourable opportunity was presented in the arrival of the Queen of Navarre, Marguerite of Valois, at Namur, on her way to Spa. The prince, numerously attended, hastened to the former town under pretence of paying his respects to the queen.

As soon as she left the place, he repaired to the glacis of the town, as if for the mere enjoyment of a walk, admired the external appearance of the citadel, and expressed a desire to be admitted inside. The young

Count of Berlaimont, in the absence of his father, the governor of the place, and an accomplice in the plot with Don John, freely admitted him. The prince immediately drew forth a pistol, and exclaimed, that "that was the first moment of his government;" took possession of the place with his immediate guard, and instantly formed them into a devoted garrison.

The Prince of Orange immediately made public the intercepted letters; and, at the solicitation of the states-general, repaired to Brussels; into which city he made a truly triumphant entry on the 23rd of September, and was immediately nominated governor, protector or *ruward* of Brabant—a dignity which had fallen into disuse, but was revived on this occasion, and which was little inferior in power to that of the dictators of Rome. (Vandervynct.) His authority, now almost unlimited, extended over every province of the Netherlands, except Namur and Luxembourg, both of which acknowledged Don John.

The first care of the liberated nation was to demolish the various citadels rendered celebrated and odious by the excesses of the Spaniards. This was done with an enthusiastic industry in which every age and sex bore a part, and which promised well for liberty. Among the ruins of that of Antwerp the statue of the Duke of Alva was discovered; dragged through the filthiest streets of the town; and, with all the indignity so well merited by the original, it was finally broken into a thousand pieces.

The country, in conferring such extensive powers on the Prince of Orange, had certainly gone too far, not for his desert, but for its own tranquillity. It was impossible that such an elevation should not excite the discontent and awaken the enmity of the haughty aristocracy of Flanders and Brabant; and particularly of the house of Croi, the ancient rivals of that of Nassau. The then representative of that family seemed the person most suited to counterbalance William's excessive power. The Duke of Arschot was therefore named Governor of Flanders; and he immediately put himself at the head of a confederacy of the Catholic party, which quickly decided to offer the chief government of the country, still in the name of Philip, to the Archduke Mathias, brother of the Emperor Rodolf II., and cousin-german to Philip of Spain, a youth but nineteen years of age.

A Flemish gentleman named Maelsted was intrusted with the proposal. Mathias joyously consented; and, quitting Vienna with the greatest secrecy, he arrived at Maestricht, without any previous announcement, and expected only by the party that had invited him, at the end of October, 1577.

The Prince of Orange, instead of showing the least symptom of dissatisfaction at this underhand proceeding aimed at his personal authority, announced his perfect approval of the nomination, and was the foremost in recommending measures for the honour of the archduke and the security of the country. He drew up the basis of a treaty for Mathias's acceptance, on terms which guaranteed to the council of state and the states-general the virtual sovereignty, and left to the young prince little beyond the fine title which had dazzled his boyish vanity. The Prince of Orange was appointed his lieutenant, in all the branches of the administration, civil, military, or financial; and the Duke of Arschot, who had hoped to obtain an entire domination over the puppet he had brought upon the stage, saw himself totally foiled in his project, and left without a chance or a pretext for the least increase to his influence.

But a still greater disappointment attended this ambitious nobleman in the very strong-hold of his power. The Flemings, driven by persecution to a state of fury almost unnatural, had, in their antipathy to Spain, adopted a hatred against Catholicism, which had its source only in political frenzy, while the converts imagined it to arise from reason and conviction. Two men had taken advantage of this state of the public mind, and gained over it an unbounded ascendency. They were Francis de Kethulle Lord of Ryhove, and John Hembyse, who each seemed formed to realise the *beau-ideal* of a factious demagogue. They had acquired supreme power over the people of Ghent, and had at their command a body of 20,000 resolute and well-armed supporters. The Duke of Arschot vainly attempted to oppose his authority to that of these men; and he on one occasion imprudently exclaimed, that:

He would have them hanged, even though they were protected by the Prince of Orange himself.

The same night Ryhove summoned the leaders of his bands; and quickly assembling a considerable force, they repaired to the duke's hotel, made him prisoner, and, without allowing him time to dress, carried him away in triumph. At the same time the bishops of Bruges and Ypres, the high bailiffs of Ghent and Courtrai, the Governor of Oudenarde, and other important magistrates, were arrested—accused of complicity with the duke, but of what particular offence the lawless demagogues did not deign to specify. The two tribunes immediately divided the whole honours and authority of administration; Ryhove as military, and Hembyse as civil, chief

The latter of these legislators completely changed the forms of the government; he revived the ancient privileges destroyed by Charles V., and took all preliminary measures for forcing the various provinces to join with the city of Ghent in forming a federative republic. The states-general and the Prince of Orange were alarmed, lest these troubles might lead to a renewal of the anarchy from the effects of which the country had but just obtained breathing-time. Ryhove consented, at the remonstrance of the Prince of Orange, to release the Duke of Arschot; but William was obliged to repair to Ghent in person, in the hope of establishing order.

He arrived on the 29th of December, and entered on a strict inquiry with his usual calmness and decision. He could not succeed in obtaining the liberty of the other prisoners, though he pleaded for them strongly. Having severely reprimanded the factious leaders, and pointed out the dangers of their illegal course, he returned to Brussels, leaving the factious city in a temporary tranquillity which his firmness and discretion could alone have obtained. (Vandervynct.)

The Archduke Mathias, having visited Antwerp, and acceded to all the conditions required of him, made his public entry into Brussels on the 18th of January, 1578, and was installed in his dignity of governor-general amidst the usual *fêtes* and rejoicings. Don John of Austria was at the same time declared an enemy to the country, with a public order to quit it without delay; and a prohibition was issued against any inhabitant acknowledging his forfeited authority.

War was now once more openly declared; some fruitless negotiations having afforded a fair pretext for hostilities. The rapid appearance of a numerous army under the orders of Don John gave strength to the suspicions of his former dissimulation. It was currently believed that large bodies of the Spanish troops had remained concealed in the forests of Luxembourg and Lorraine; while several regiments which had remained in France in the service of the League, immediately re-entered the Netherlands. Alexander Farnese Prince of Parma, son of the former *governant*, came to the aid of his uncle Don John at the head of a large force of Italians; and these several reinforcements, with the German auxiliaries still in the country, composed an army of 20,000 men. (Vandervynct.) The army of the states-general was still larger; but far inferior in point of discipline. It was commanded by Antoine de Goignies, a gentleman of Hainault, and an old soldier of the school of Charles V.

After a sharp affair at the village of Riminants, in which the royalists had the worst, the two armies met at Gemblours, on the 31st of January, 1578; and the Prince of Parma gained a complete victory, almost with his cavalry only, taking De Goignies prisoner, with the whole of his artillery and baggage. (Bentivoglio.) The account of his victory is almost miraculous. The royalists, if we are to credit their most minute but not impartial historian, had only 1200 men engaged; by whom 6000 were put to the sword, with the loss of but twelve men and little more than an hour's labour. (Strada.)

The news of this battle threw the states into the utmost consternation. Brussels being considered insecure, the Archduke Mathias and his council retired to Antwerp; but the victors did not feel their forces sufficient to justify an attack upon the capital. They, however, took Louvain, Tirlemont, and several other towns; but these conquests were of little import in comparison with the loss of Amsterdam, which declared openly and unanimously for the patriot cause. The states-general recovered their courage, and prepared for a new contest. They sent deputies to the *diet* of Worms, to ask succour from the princes of the empire. The count palatine John Casimir repaired to their assistance with a considerable force of Germans and English, all equipped and paid by Queen Elizabeth. (Vandervynct.) The Duke of Alençon, brother of Henry III. of France, hovered on the frontiers of Hainault with a respectable army; and the cause of liberty seemed not quite desperate.

But all the various chiefs had separate interests and opposite views; while the fanatic violence of the people of Ghent sapped the foundations of the pacification to which the town had given its name. The Walloon provinces, deep-rooted in their attachment to religious bigotry, which they loved still better than political freedom, gradually withdrew from the common cause; and without yet openly becoming reconciled with Spain, they adopted a neutrality which was tantamount to it Don John was, however, deprived of all chance of reaping any advantage from these unfortunate dissensions. He was suddenly taken ill in his camp at Bougy; and died, after a fortnight's suffering, on the 1st of October, 1578, in the 33rd year of his age. (Vandervynct.)

This unlooked-for close to a career which had been so brilliant, and to a life from which so much was yet to be expected, makes us pause to consider for a moment the different opinions of his times and of history on the fate of a personage so remarkable. The contemporary Flemish memoirs say that he died of the plague; those of Spain call his disorder the purple fever. The examination of his corpse caused an almost general belief that he was poisoned. One author (Herrera) says:

He lost his life, with great suspicion of poison.

Another (Cabrera) speaks of the suspicious state of his intestines, but without any direct opinion. An English historian (Hume) states the fact of his being poisoned, without any reserve. Flemish writers do not hesitate to attribute his murder to the jealousy of Philip II., who, they assert, had discovered a secret treaty of marriage about to be concluded between Don John and Elizabeth of England, securing them the joint sovereignty of the Netherlands. (See Vandervynct.) An Italian historian (Bentivoglio) of credit asserts that this ambitious design was attributed to the prince; and admits that his death was not considered as having arisen from natural causes.

It was also believed that Escovedo, his confidential secretary, being immediately called back to Spain, was secretly assassinated by Antonio Perez, Philip's celebrated minister, and by the special orders of the king. Time has, however, covered the affair with impenetrable mystery; and the death of Don John was of little importance to the affairs of the country he governed so briefly and so ingloriously, if it be not that it added another motive to the natural hatred for his assumed murderer.

The Prince of Parma, who now succeeded, by virtue of Don John's testament, to the post of governor-general in the name of the king, remained intrenched in his camp. He expected much from the disunion of his various opponents; and what he foresaw, very quickly happened. The Duke of Alençon disbanded his troops and returned to France; and the prince palatine, following his example, withdrew to Germany, having first made an unsuccessful attempt to engage the Queen of England as a principal in the confederacy. In this perplexity, the Prince of Orange saw that the real hope for safety was in uniting still more closely the northern provinces of the union; for he discovered the fallacy of reckoning on the cordial and persevering fidelity of the Walloons.

He therefore convoked a new assembly at Utrecht; and the deputies of Holland, Guelders, Zealand, Utrecht, and Groningen, signed, on the 29th of January, 1579, the famous act called the *Union of Utrecht*, the real basis or fundamental pact of the republic of the United Provinces. It makes no formal renunciation of allegiance to Spain, but this is virtually done by the omission of the king's name. The twenty-six articles of this act consolidate the indissoluble connexion of the United Provinces; each preserving its separate franchises, and following, its own good pleasure on the subject of religion. The towns of Ghent, Antwerp, Bruges, and Ypres, soon after acceded to and joined the union.

The Prince of Parma now assumed the offensive, and marched against Maestricht with his whole army. He took, the place in the month of June, 1579, after a gallant resistance, and delivered it to sack and massacre for three entire days. About the same time Mechlin and Bois-le-duc returned to their obedience to the king. Hembyse having renewed his attempts against the public peace at Ghent, the Prince of Orange repaired to that place with speed; and having re-established order, and frightened the inveterate demagogue into secret flight, Flanders was once more restored to tranquillity.

An attempt was made this year at a reconciliation between the king and the states. The emperor Rodolf II. and Pope Gregory XIII. offered their mediation; and on the 5th of April a congress assembled at Cologne, where a number of the most celebrated diplomatists in Europe were collected. (Vandervynct.) But it was early seen that no settlement would result from the apparently reciprocal wish for peace. One point—that of religion, the main, and indeed the only one in debate—was now maintained by Philip's ambassador in the same unchristian spirit, as if torrents of blood and millions of treasure had never been sacrificed in the cause. Philip was inflexible in his resolution never to concede the exercise of the reformed worship; and after nearly a year of fruitless consultation, and the expenditure of immense sums of money, the congress separated on the 17th of November, without having effected anything. There were several other articles intended for discussion, had the main one been adjusted, on which Philip was fully as determined to make no concession; but his obstinacy was not put to these new tests.

The time had now arrived for the execution of the great and decisive step for independence, the means of effecting which had been so long the object of exertion and calculation on the part of the Prince of Orange. He now resolved to assemble the states of the United Provinces, solemnly abjure the dominion of Spain, and depose King Philip from the sovereignty he had so justly forfeited. Much has been written both for and against this measure, which involved every argument of natural rights and municipal privilege. The natural rights of man may seem to comprise only those which he enjoys in a state of nature: but he carries several of those with him into society, which is based upon the very principle of their preservation. The great precedent which so many subsequent revolutions have acknowledged and confirmed, is that which we now record.

The states-general assembled at Antwerp early in the year 1580; and, in spite of all the opposition of the Catholic deputies, the authority of Spain was revoked for ever, and the United Provinces declared a free and independent state. At the same time was debated the important question as to whether the protection of the new state should be offered to England or to France. Opinions were divided on this point; but that of the Prince of Orange being in favour of the latter country, from many motives of sound policy, it was decided to offer the sovereignty to the Duke of Alençon.

The Archduke Mathias, who was present at the deliberations, was treated with little ceremony; but he obtained the promise of a pension when the finances were in a situation to afford it. The definite proposal to be made to the Duke of Alençon was not agreed upon for some months afterwards; and it was in the month of August Allowing that St Aldegonde and other deputies waited on the duke at the *château* of Plessis-le-Tours, when he accepted the offered sovereignty on the proposed conditions, which set narrow bounds to his authority, and gave ample security to the United Provinces. (Vandervynct)

The articles were formally signed on the 29th day of September; and the duke not only promised quickly to lead a numerous army to the Netherlands, but he obtained a letter from his brother Henry III., dated December 26th, by which the king pledged himself to give further aid, as soon as he might succeed in quieting his own disturbed and unfortunate country. The states-general, assembled at Delft, ratified the treaty on the 30th of December; and the year which was about to open seemed to promise the consolidation of freedom and internal peace.

CHAPTER 6

1580–1584

TO THE MURDER OF THE PRINCE OF ORANGE

Philip might be well excused the utmost violence of resentment on this occasion, had it been bounded by fair and honourable efforts for the maintenance of his authority. But every general principle seemed lost in the base inveteracy of private hatred. The ruin of the Prince of Orange was his main object, and his industry and ingenuity were taxed to the utmost to procure his murder. (D'Ewez, *Hist. Gen. des Pays Bas*, t. vi.) Existing documents prove that he first wished to accomplish this in such a way as that the responsibility and odium of the act might rest on the Prince of Parma; but the mind of the prince was at that period too magnanimous to allow of a participation in the crime. The correspondence on the subject is preserved in the archives, and the date of Philip's first letter (30th of November, 1579,) proves that even before the final disavowal of his authority by the United Provinces, he had harboured his diabolical design. The prince remonstrated, but with no effect. It even appears that Philip's anxiety would not admit of the delay necessary for the prince's reply. The infamous edict of proscription against William bears date the 15th of March; and the most pressing letters commanded the Prince of Parma to make it public. It was not, however, till the 15th of June that he sent forth the fatal ban.

This edict, under Philip's own signature, is a tissue of invective and virulence. The illustrious object of its abuse is accused of having engaged the heretics to profane the churches and break the images; of having persecuted and massacred the Catholic priests; of hypocrisy, tyranny, and perjury; and, as the height of atrocity, of having introduced liberty of conscience into his country! For these causes, and many others, the king declares him "proscribed and banished as a public pest;" and it is permitted to all persons to assail him "in his fortune, person, and life, as an enemy to human nature." Philip also, "for the recompense of virtue and the punishment of crime," promises to whoever will deliver up William of Nassau, dead or alive, "in lands or money, at his choice, the sum of 25,000 golden crowns; to grant a free pardon to such person for all former offences of what kind soever, and to invest him with letters patent of nobility."

In reply to this brutal document of human depravity, William published all over Europe his famous "Apology;" of which it is enough to say, that language could not produce a more splendid refutation of every charge, or a more terrible recrimination against the guilty tyrant. It was attributed to the pen of Peter de Villiers, a Protestant minister. It is universally pronounced one of the noblest monuments of history. (Voltaire.) William, from the hour of his proscription, became at once the equal in worldly station, as he had ever been the superior in moral worth, of his royal calumniator. He took his place as a prince of an imperial family, not less ancient or illustrious than that of the house of Austria; and he stood forward at the supreme tribunal of public feeling and opinion as the accuser of a king who disgraced his lineage and his throne.

By a separate article in the treaty with the states, the Duke of Alençon secured to William the sovereignty of Holland and Zealand, as well as the lordship of Friesland, with his title of *stadtholder*, retaining to the duke his claim on the prince's faith and homage. (Meteren.) The exact nature of William's authority was finally ratified on the 24th of July, 1561; on which day he took the prescribed oath, and entered on the exercise of his well-earned rights.

Philip now formed the design of sending back the Duchess of Parma to resume her former situation as *governant*, and exercise the authority conjointly with her son. But the latter positively declined this proposal of divided power; and he, consequently, was left alone to its entire exercise. Military affairs made but slow progress this year. The most remarkable event was the capture of La Noue, a native of Bretagne, one of the bravest, and certainly the cleverest, officers in the service of the states, into which he had passed after having given important aid to the Huguenots of France. He was considered so important a prize, that Philip refused all proposals for his exchange, and detained him in the castle of Limbourg for five years.

The siege of Cambray was now undertaken by the Prince of

Parma in person; while the Duke of Alençon, at the head of a large army, and the flower of the French nobility, advanced to its relief, and soon forced his rival to raise the siege. The new sovereign of the Netherlands entered the town, and was received with tumultuous joy by the half-starved citizens and garrison. The Prince of Parma sought an equivalent for this check in the attack of Tournay, which he immediately afterwards invested. The town was but feebly garrisoned; but the Protestant inhabitants prepared for a desperate defence, under the exciting example of the Princess of Epinoi, wife of the governor, who was himself absent. This remarkable woman furnishes another proof of the female heroism which abounded in these wars.

Though wounded in the arm, she fought in the breach sword in hand, braving peril and death. And when at length it was impossible to hold out longer, she obtained an honourable capitulation, and marched out, on the 29th of November, on horseback, at the head of the garrison, with an air of triumph rather than of defeat.

The Duke of Alençon, now created Duke of Anjou, by which title we shall hereafter distinguish him, had repaired to England, in hopes of completing his project of marriage with Elizabeth. After three months of almost confident expectation, the virgin queen, at this time fifty years of age, with a caprice not quite justifiable, broke all her former engagements; and, happily for herself and her country, declined the marriage. Anjou burst out into all the violence of his turbulent temper, and set sail for the Netherlands. (Camden.) Elizabeth made all the reparation in her power, by the honours paid him on his dismissal. She accompanied him as far as Canterbury, and sent him away under the convoy of the Earl of Leicester, her chief favourite; and with a brilliant suite and a fleet of fifteen sail. Anjou was received at Antwerp with equid distinction; and was inaugurated there on the 19th of February as Duke of Brabant, Lothier, Limbourg, and Guelders, with many other titles, of which he soon proved himself unworthy. When the Prince of Orange, at the ceremony, placed the ducal mantle on his shoulders, Anjou said to him, "Fasten it so well, prince, that they cannot take it off again!"

During the rejoicings which followed this inauspicious ceremony, Philip's proscription against the Prince of Orange put forth its first fruits. The latter gave a grand dinner in the *château* of Antwerp, which he occupied, on the 18th of March, the birthday of the Duke of Anjou; and, as he was quitting the dining-room, on his way to his private chamber, a young man stepped forward and offered a pretended petition, William being at all times of easy access for such an object. While he read the paper, the treacherous suppliant discharged a pistol at his head: the ball struck him under the left ear, and passed out at the right cheek. As he tottered and fell, the assassin drew a poniard to add suicide to the crime, but he was instantly put to death by the attendant guards.

The young Count Maurice, William's second son, examined the murderer's body; and the papers found on him, and subsequent inquiries, told fully who and what he was. His name was John Jaureguay, his age twenty-three years; he was a native of Biscay, and clerk to a Spanish merchant of Antwerp, called Gaspar Anastro. This man had instigated him to the crime; having received a promise signed by King Philip, engaging to give him 28,000 *ducats* and other advantages, if he would undertake to assassinate the Prince of Orange. (Meteren, De Thou, &c.) The inducements held out by Anastro to his simple dupe, were backed strongly by the persuasions of Antony Timmerman, a Dominican monk; and by Venero, Anastro's cashier, who had from fear declined becoming himself the murderer.

Jaureguay had duly heard mass, and received the sacrament, before executing his attempt; and in his pockets were found a catechism of the Jesuits, with tablets filled with prayers in the Spanish language; one in particular being addressed to the Angel Gabriel, imploring his intercession with God and the Virgin, to aid him in the consummation of his object. Other accompanying absurdities seem to pronounce this miserable wretch to be as much an instrument in the hands of others as the weapon of his crime was in his own. Timmerman and Venero made a full avowal of their criminality, and suffered death in the usual barbarous manner of the times. The Jesuits, some years afterwards, solemnly gathered the remains of these three pretended martyrs, and exposed them as holy relics for public veneration. (D'Ewez.) Anastro effected his escape.

The alarm and indignation of the people of Antwerp knew no bounds. Their suspicions at first fell on the Duke of Anjou and the French party; but the truth was soon discovered; and the rapid recovery of the Prince of Orange from his desperate wound, set everything once more to rights. But a premature report of his death flew rapidly abroad; and he had anticipated proofs of his importance in the eyes of all Europe, in the frantic, delight of the base, and the deep affliction of the good. Within three months, William was able to accompany the Duke of Anjou in his visits to Ghent, Bruges, and the other chief towns of Flanders; in each of which the ceremony of inauguration was repeated. Several military exploits now took place, and various towns fell into the hands of the opposing parties; changing masters with a rapidity, as well as a previous endurance of suffering, that must have carried confusion and change on the contending principles of allegiance into the hearts and heads of the harassed inhabitants.

The Duke of Anjou, intemperate, inconstant, and unprincipled, saw that his authority was but the shadow of power, compared to the deep-fixed practices of despotism which governed the other nations of Europe. The French officers, who formed his suite and possessed all his confidence, had no difficulty in raising his discontent into treason against the people with whom he had made a solemn compact. The result of their councils was a deep-laid plot against Flemish liberty; and its execution was ere-long attempted. He sent secret orders to the governors of Dunkirk, Bruges, Termonde, and other towns, to seize on and hold them in his name; reserving for himself the infamy of the enterprise against Antwerp. To prepare for its execution, he caused his numerous army of French and Swiss to approach the city; and they were encamped in the neighbourhood, at a place called Borgerhout.

On the 17th of January, 1583, the duke dined somewhat earlier than usual, under the pretext of proceeding afterwards to review his army in their camp. He set out at noon, accompanied by his guard of 200 horse; and when he reached the second drawbridge, one of his officers gave the preconcerted signal for an attack on the Flemish guard, by pretending that he had fallen and broken his leg. The duke called out to his followers, "Courage, courage! the town is ours!" The guard at the gate was all soon dispatched; and the French troops, which waited outside to the number of 3000, rushed quickly in, furiously shouting the war-cry, "Town taken! town taken! kill! kill!" The astonished but intrepid citizens, recovering from their confusion, instantly flew to arms. All differences in religion or politics were forgotten in the common danger to their freedom. Catholics and Protestants, men and women, rushed alike to the conflict. The ancient spirit of Flanders seemed to animate all.

Workmen, armed with the instruments of their various trades, started from their shops and flung themselves upon the enemy. A baker sprang from the cellar where he was kneading his dough, and with his oven shovel struck a French dragoon to the ground. Those who had fire-arms, after expending their bullets, took from their pouches and pockets pieces of money, which they bent between their teeth, and used for charging their arquebusses. The French were driven successively from the streets and ramparts, and the cannons planted on the latter were immediately turned against the reinforcements which attempted to enter the town. The French were everywhere beaten; the Duke of Anjou saved himself by flight, and reached Termonde, after the perilous necessity of passing through a large tract of inundated country. His loss in this base enterprise amounted to 1500; while that of the citizens did not exceed eighty men. (Meteren.) The attempts simultaneously made on the other towns succeeded at Dunkirk and Termonde; but all the others failed.

The character of the Prince of Orange never appeared so thoroughly great as at this crisis. With wisdom and magnanimity rarely equalled and never surpassed, he threw himself and his authority between the indication of the country and the guilt of Anjou; saving the former from excess, and the latter from execration. The disgraced and discomfited duke proffered to the states excuses as mean as they were hypocritical; and his brother, the King of France, sent a special envoy to intercede for him. But it was the influence of William that screened the culprit from public reprobation and ruin, and regained for him the place and power which he might easily have secured for himself, had he not prized the welfare of his country far above all objects of private advantage.

A new treaty was negotiated, confirming Anjou in his former station, with renewed security against any future treachery on his part. He in the meantime retired to France, to let the public indignation subside; but before he could assume sufficient confidence again to face the country he had so basely injured, his worthless existence was suddenly terminated, some thought by poison—the common solution of all such doubtful questions in those days—in the month of June in the following year. He expired in his twenty-ninth year.

A disgusting proof of public ingratitude and want of judgment was previously furnished by the conduct of the people of Antwerp against him who had been so often their deliverer from such various dangers. Unable to comprehend the greatness of his mind, they openly accused the Prince of Orange of having joined with the French for their subjugation, and of having concealed a body of that detested nation in the citadel. The populace rushed to the place, and having minutely examined it, were convinced of their own absurdity and the prince's innocence. He scorned to demand their punishment for such an outrageous calumny; but he was not the less afflicted, at it.

(D'Ewez.) He took the resolution of quitting Flanders, as it turned out, for ever; and he retired into Zealand, where he was better known and consequently better trusted.

In the midst of the consequent confusion in the former of these provinces, the Prince of Parma with indefatigable vigour, made himself master of town after town; and turned his particular attention to the creation of a naval force, which was greatly favoured by the possession of Dunkirk, Nieuport, and Gravelines. Native treachery was not idle in this time of tumult and confusion. The count of Renneberg, Governor of Friesland and Groningen, had set the basest example, and gone over to the Spaniards. The Prince of Chimay, son of the Duke of Arschot, and Governor of Bruges, yielded to the persuasions of his father, and gave up the place to the Prince of Parma. Hembyse also, amply confirming the bad opinion in which the Prince of Orange always held him, returned to Ghent, where he regained a great portion of his former influence, and immediately commenced a correspondence with the Prince of Parma, offering to deliver up both Ghent and Termonde. An attempt was consequently made by the Spaniards to surprise the former town; but the citizens were prepared for this, having intercepted some of the letters of Hembyse; and the traitor was seized, tried, condemned, and executed on the 4th of August, 1564. He was upwards of seventy years of age. (Vandervynct.) Ryhove, his celebrated colleague, died in Holland some years later. But the fate of so insignificant a person as Hembyse passed almost unnoticed, in the agitation caused by an event which shortly preceded his death.

From the moment of their abandonment by the Duke of Anjou, the United Provinces considered themselves independent; and although they consented to renew his authority over the country at large, at the solicitation of the Prince of Orange, they were resolved to confirm the influence of the latter over their particular interests, which they were now sensible could acquire stability only by that means. (Meteren.) The death of Anjou left them without a sovereign; and they did not hesitate in the choice which they were now called upon to make.

On whom, indeed, could they fix but William of Nassau, without the utmost injustice to him, and the deepest injury to themselves? To whom could they turn, in preference to him who had given consistency to the early explosion of their despair; to him who first gave the country political existence, then nursed it into freedom, and now beheld it in the vigour and prime of independence? He had seen the necessity, but certainly over-rated the value, of foreign support, to enable the new state to cope with the tremendous tyranny from which it had broken. He had tried successively Germany, England, and France.

From the first and the last of these powers he had received two governors, to whom he cheerfully resigned the title. The incapacity of both, and the treachery of the latter, proved to the states that their only chance for safety was in the consolidation of William's authority; and they contemplated the noblest reward which a grateful nation could bestow on a glorious liberator. And is it to be believed, that he who for twenty years had sacrificed his repose, lavished his fortune, and risked his life, for the public cause, now aimed at absolute dominion, or coveted a despotism which all his actions prove him to have abhorred? Defeated bigotry has put forward such vapid accusations. He has been also held responsible for the early cruelties which, it is notorious, he used every means to avert, and frequently punished. But while these revolting acts can only be viewed in the light of reprisals against the bloodiest persecution that ever existed, by exasperated men driven to vengeance by a bad example, not one single act of cruelty or bad faith has ever been made good against William, who may be safely renounced one of the wisest and best men that history has held up as examples to the species.

The authority of one author has been produced to prove that, during the lifetime of his brother Louis, offers were made to him by France, of the sovereignty of the northern provinces, on condition of the southern being joined to the French crown. (Amelot de la Houssaye.) That he ever accepted those offers is without proof: that he never acted on them is certain. But he might have been justified in purchasing freedom for those states which had so well earned it, at the price even of a qualified independence under another power, to the exclusion of those which had never heartily struggled against Spain.

The best evidence, however, of William's real views is to be found in the Capitulation, as it is called; that is to say, the act which was on the point of being executed between him and the states, when a base fanatic, instigated by a bloody tyrant, put a period to his splendid career. This capitulation exists at full length, (Bor. *liv*.15), but was never formally executed. Its conditions are founded on the same principles, and conceived in nearly the same terms, as those accepted by the Duke of Anjou; and the whole compact is one of the most thoroughly liberal that history has on record. The prince repaired to Delft for the ceremony of his inauguration, the price of his long labours; but there, instead of anticipated dignity, he met the sudden stroke of death. (Grotius.)

On the 10th of July, as he left his dining-room, and while he placed his foot on the first step of the great stair leading to the upper apartments of his house, a man named Balthazar Gerard, (who, like the former assassin, waited for him at the moment of convivial relaxation,) discharged a pistol at his body: three balls entered it. He fell into the arms of an attendant, and cried out faintly, in the French language, "God pity me! I am sadly wounded—God have mercy on my soul, and on this unfortunate nation!" His sister, the countess of Swartzenberg, who now hastened to his side, asked him in German, if he did not recommend his soul to God?

He answered, "Yes," in the same language, but with a feeble voice. He was carried into the dining-room, where he immediately expired. His sister closed his eyes (La Pise, *Hist, des Princes d'Orange*): his wife, too, was on the spot—Louisa, daughter of the illustrious Coligny, and widow of the gallant Count of Teligny, both of whom were also murdered almost in her sight, in the frightful massacre of St Bartholomew. We may not enter on a description of the afflicting scene which followed: but the mind is pleased in picturing the bold solemnity with which Prince Maurice, then eighteen years of age, swore—not vengeance or hatred against his father's murderers—but that he would faithfully and religiously follow the glorious example he had given him.

******

Whoever would really enjoy the spirit of historical details should never omit an opportunity of seeing places rendered memorable by associations connected with the deeds, and especially with the death, of great men; the spot, for instance, where William was assassinated at Delft; the old staircase he was just on the point of ascending; the narrow pass between that and the dining-hall whence he came out, of scarcely sufficient extent for the murderer to hold forth his arm and his pistol, 2½ feet long. This weapon, and its fellow, are both preserved in the museum of The Hague, together with two of the fatal bullets, and the very clothes which the victim wore. The leathern doublet, pierced by the balls and burned by the powder, lies beside the other parts of the dress, the simple gravity of which, ill fashion and colour, irresistibly brings the wise, great man before us, and adds a hundred-fold to the interest excited by a recital of his murder.

★★★★★★

There is but one important feature in the character of William which we have hitherto left untouched, but which the circumstances of his death seemed to sanctify, and point out for record in the same page with it. We mean, his religious opinions; and we shall dispatch a subject which is, in regard to all men, so delicate, indeed so sacred, in a few words. He was born a Lutheran. When he arrived, a boy, at the court of Charles V., he was initiated into the Catholic creed, in which he was thenceforward brought up. Afterwards, when he could think for himself and choose his profession of faith, he embraced the doctrine of Calvin. His whole public conduct seems to prove that he viewed sectarian principles chiefly in the light or political instruments; and that, himself a conscientious Christian, in the broad sense of the term, he was deeply imbued with the spirit of universal toleration, and considered the various shades of belief as subservient to the one grand principle of civil and religious liberty, for which he had long devoted and at length laid down his life.

His assassin was taken alive, and four days afterwards executed with terrible circumstances of cruelty, which he bore as a martyr might have borne them. (Le Petit, *Histoire des Pays Bas*.) He was a native of Burgundy, and had for some months lingered near his victim, and insinuated himself into his confidence by a feigned attachment to liberty, and an apparent zeal for the reformed faith. He was nevertheless a bigoted Catholic; and, by his own confession, he had communicated his design to, and received encouragement to its execution from, more than one minister of the sect to which he belonged. But his avowal criminated a more important accomplice, and one whose character stands so high in history, that it behoves us to examine thoroughly the truth of the accusation, and the nature of the collateral proofs by which it is supported.

Most writers on this question have leaned to the side which all would wish to adopt, for the honour of human nature and the integrity of a celebrated name. But an original letter exists in the archives of Brussels, from the Prince of Parma himself to Philip of Spain, in which he admits that Balthazar Gerard had communicated to him his intention of murdering the Prince of Orange, some months before the deed was done; and he mixes phrases of compassion for "the poor man" (the murderer) and of praise for the act; which, if the document be really authentic, sinks Alexander of Parma as low as the wretch with whom he sympathized. (See D'Ewez, *Hist. Gen. de la Belgique*, t. vi.)

CHAPTER 7

1584–1592

TO THE DEATH OF ALEXANDER PRINCE OF PARMA

The death of William of Nassau not only closes the scene of his individual career, but throws a deep gloom over the history of a revolution that was sealed by so great a sacrifice. The animation of the story seems suspended. Its events lose for a time their excitement' The last act of the political drama is performed. The great hero of the tragedy is no more. The other most memorable actors have one by one passed away. A whole generation has fallen in the contest; and it is with exhausted interest, and feelings less intense, that we resume the details of war and blood, which seem no longer sanctified by the grander movements of heroism. The stirring impulse of slavery breaking its chains yields to the colder inspiration of independence maintaining its rights. The men we have now to depict were born free; and the deeds they did were those of stern resolve rather than of frantic despair. The present picture may be as instructive as the last, but it is less thrilling. Passion gives place to reason; and that which wore the air of fierce romance is superseded by what bears the stamp of calm reality.

The consternation caused by the news of William's death soon yielded to the firmness natural to a people inured to suffering and calamity. The United Provinces rejected at once the overtures made by the Prince of Parma to induce them to obedience. They seemed proud to show that their fate did not depend on that of one man. He therefore turned his attention to the most effective means of obtaining results by force, which he found it impossible to secure by persuasion. He proceeded vigorously to the reduction of the chief towns of Flanders, the conquest of which would give him possession of the entire province, no army now remaining to oppose him in the field.

He soon obliged Ypres and Termonde to surrender; and Ghent, forced by famine, at length yielded on reasonable terms. The most severe was the utter abolition of the reformed religion; by which a large portion of the population was driven to the alternative of exile; and they passed over in crowds to Holland and Zealand, not half of the inhabitants remaining behind. Mechlin, and finally Brussels, worn out by a fruitless resistance, followed the example of the rest; and thus, within a year after the death of William of Nassau, the power of Spain was again established in the whole province of Flanders, and the others which comprise what is in modern days generally denominated Belgium.

But these domestic victories of the Prince of Parma were barren in any of those results which humanity would love to see in the train of conquest. The reconciled provinces presented the most deplorable spectacle. The chief towns were almost depopulated. The inhabitants had in a great measure fallen victims to war, pestilence, and famine. Little inducement existed to replace by marriage the ravages caused by death, for few men wished to propagate a race which divine wrath seemed to have marked for persecution. The thousands of villages which had covered the face of the country were absolutely abandoned to the wolves, which had so rapidly increased, that they attacked not merely cattle and children, but grown-up persons. The dogs, driven abroad by hunger, had become as ferocious as other beasts of prey, and joined in large packs to hunt down brutes and men.

Neither fields, nor woods, nor roads, were now to be distinguished by any visible limits. All was an entangled mass of trees, weeds, and grass. The prices of the necessaries of life were so high, that people of rank, after selling everything to buy bread, were obliged to have recourse to open beggary in the streets of the great towns. From this frightful picture, and the numerous details which imagination may readily supply, we gladly turn to the contrast afforded by the northern states. Those we have just described have a feeble hold upon our sympathies; we cannot pronounce their sufferings to be unmerited. The want of firmness or enlightment, which preferred such an existence to the risk of entire destruction, only heightens the glory of the people whose unyielding energy and courage gained them so proud a place among the independent nations of Europe.

The murder of William seemed to carry to the United Provinces conviction of the weakness as well as the atrocity of Spain; and the indecent joy excited among the royalists added to their courage. An immediate council was created, composed of eighteen members, at the head of which was unanimously placed Prince Maurice of Nassau (who even then gave striking indications of talent and prudence); his elder brother, the Count of Beuren, now Prince of Orange, being still kept captive in Spain. Count Hohenloe was appointed lieutenant-general; and several other measures were promptly adopted to consolidate the power of the infant republic. The whole of its forces amounted but to 5500 men. The Prince of Parma had 80,000 at his command. (Hooft.) With such means of carrying on his conquests, he sat down regularly before Antwerp, and commenced the operations of one of the most celebrated among the many memorable sieves of those times.

He completely surrounded the city with troops; placing a large portion of his army on the left bank of the Scheldt, the other on the right; and causing to be attacked at the same time the two strong forts of Liefkinshoek and Lilla. Repulsed on the latter important point, his only hope of gaining the command of the navigation of the river, on which the success of the siege depended was by throwing a bridge across the stream. Neither its great rapidity, nor its immense width, nor the want of wood and workmen, could deter him from this vast undertaking. He was assisted, if not guided, in all his projects on the occasion, by Barroccio, a celebrated Italian engineer sent to him by Philip; and the merit of all that was done ought fairly to be, at least, divided between the general and the engineer. If enterprise and perseverance belonged to the first, science and skill were the portion of the latter.

They first caused two strong forts to be erected at opposite sides of the river; and adding to their resources by every possible means, they threw forward a pier on each side of, and far into, the stream. The stakes, driven firmly into the bed of the river and cemented with masses of earth and stones, were at a proper height covered with planks and defended by parapets. These *estoccades*, as they were called, reduced the river to half its original breadth; and the cannon with which they were mounted rendered the passage extremely dangerous to hostile vessels. But, to fill up this strait, a considerable number of boats were fastened together by chain-hooks and anchors; and being manned and armed with cannon, they were moored in the interval between the *estoccades*. During these operations, a canal was cut between the Moer and Calloo; by which means a communication was formed with

Ghent, which insured a supply of ammunition and provisions. The works of the bridge, which was 2400 feet in length, were constructed with such strength and solidity, that they braved the winds, the floods, and the ice of the whole winter.

The people of Antwerp at first laughed to scorn the whole of these stupendous preparations: but when they found that the bridge resisted the natural elements, by which they doubted not it would have been destroyed, they began to tremble in the anticipation of famine; yet they vigorously prepared for their defence, and rejected the overtures made by the Prince of Parma even at this advanced stage of his proceedings. Ninety-seven pieces of cannon now defended the bridge; besides which, thirty large barges at each side of the river guarded its extremities; and forty ships of war formed a fleet of protection, constantly ready to meet any attack from the besieged. They, seeing the Scheldt thus really closed up, and all communication with Zealand impossible, felt their whole safety to depend on the destruction of the bridge.

The states of Zealand now sent forward an expedition, which, joined with some ships from Lillo, gave new courage to the besieged; and everything was prepared for their great attempt. An Italian engineer named Giambelli was at this time in Antwerp, and by his talents had long protracted the defence. He has the chief merit of being the inventor of those terrible fire-ships which gained the title of "infernal machines;" and with some of these formidable instruments and the Zealand fleet, the long-projected attack was at length made.

Early on the night of the 4th of April, the Prince of Parma and his army were amazed by the spectacle of three huge masses of flame floating down the river, accompanied by numerous lesser appearances of a similar kind, and bearing directly against the prodigious barrier, which had cost months of labour to him and his troops, and immense sums of money to the state. The whole surface of the Scheldt presented one sheet of fire; the country all round was as visible as at noon; the flags, the arms of the soldiers, and every object on the bridge, in the fleet, or the forts, stood out clearly to view; and the pitchy darkness of the sky gave increased effect to the marked distinctness of all.

Astonishment was soon succeeded by consternation, when one of the three machines burst with a terrific noise before they reached their intended mark, but time enough to offer a sample of their nature. The Prince of Parma, with numerous officers and soldiers rushed to the bridge, to witness the effects of this explosion; and just then a second and still larger fire-ship, having burst through the flying bridge of boats, struck against one of the *estoccades*. Alexander, unmindful of danger, used every exertion of his authority to stimulate the sailors in their attempts to clear away the monstrous machine which threatened destruction to all within its reach. Happily, for him, an ensign who was near, forgetting in his general's peril all rules of discipline and forms of ceremony, actually forced him from the *estoccade*. He had not put his foot on the river bank when the machine blew up. The effects were such as really baffle description. The bridge was burst through; the *estoccade* was shattered almost to atoms, and, with all that it supported—men, cannon, and the huge machinery employed in the various works—dispersed in the air.

The cruel Marquis of Roubais, many other officers, and 800 soldiers, perished, in all varieties of death—by flood, or flame, or the horrid wounds from the missiles with which the terrible machine was overcharged. Fragments of bodies and limbs were flung far. and wide; and many gallant soldiers were destroyed, without a vestige of the human form being left to prove that they had ever existed. The river, forced from its bed at either side, rushed into the forts and drowned numbers of their garrisons; while the ground far beyond shook as in an earthquake. (Bentivoglio, Schiller, Vandervynct, and Strada).

The prince was struck down by a beam, and lay for some time senseless, together with two generals, Delvasto and Gajitani, both more seriously wounded than he; and many of the soldiers were burned and mutilated in the most frightful manner. Alexander soon recovered; and by his presence of mind, humanity, and resolution, he endeavoured with incredible quickness to repair the mischief, and raised the confidence of his army as high as ever. Had the Zealand fleet come in time to the spot, the whole plan might have been crowned with success; but by some want of concert, or accidental delay, it did not appear; and consequently, the beleaguered town received no relief.

One last resource was left to the besieged; that which had formerly been resorted to at Leyden, and by which the place was saved. To enable them to inundate the immense plain which stretched between Lillo and Strabrock up to the walls of Antwerp, it was necessary to cut through the dike which defended it against the irruptions of the eastern Scheldt. This plain was traversed by a high and wide counter-dike, called the dike of Couvestien, and Alexander, knowing its importance, had early taken possession of and strongly defended it by several forts. Two attacks were made by the garrison of Antwerp on this important construction; the latter of which led to one of the most desperate encounters of the war. The prince, seeing that on the results of this day depended the whole consequences of his labours, fought with a valour, that even he had never before displayed, and he was finally victorious. The confederates were forced to abandon the attack, leaving 3000 dead upon the dike or at its base; and the Spaniards lost full 800 men.

One more fruitless attempt was made to destroy the bridge and raise the siege, by means of an enormous vessel bearing the presumptuous title of *The End of the War*. But this floating citadel ran aground, without producing any effect; and the gallant Governor of Antwerp, the celebrated Philip de Saint Aldegonde, was forced to capitulate on the 16th of August, after a siege of fourteen months. The reduction of Antwerp was compered a miracle of perseverance and courage. The Prince of Parma was elevated by his success to the highest pinnacle of renown; and Philip, on receiving the news, displayed a burst of joy such as rarely varied his cold and gloomy reserve.

Even while the fate of Antwerp was undecided, the United Provinces, seeing that they were still too weak to resist alone the undivided force of the Spanish monarchy, had opened negotiations with France and England at once, in the hope of gaining one or the other for an ally and protector. Henry III. gave a most honourable reception to the ambassadors sent to his court, and was evidently disposed to accept their offers, had not the distracted state of his own country, still torn by civil war, quite disabled him from any effective co-operation. The deputies sent to England were also well received.

Elizabeth listened to the proposals of the states, sent them an ambassador in return, and held out the most flattering hopes of succour. But her cautious policy would not suffer her to accept the sovereignty; and she declared that she would in no ways interfere with the negotiations, which might end in its being accepted by the King of France. (Meteren.) She gave prompt evidence of her sincerity by an advance of considerable sums of money, and by sending to Holland a body of 6000 troops, under the command of her favourite, Robert Dudley Earl of Leicester; and as security for the repayment of her loan, the towns of Flushing and Brille, and the castle of Rammekins, were given up to her. (Hume vol. v.)

The Earl of Leicester was accompanied by a splendid retinue of noblemen, and a select troop of 500 followers. He was received at Flushing by the governor, Sir Philip Sidney, his nephew, the model of manners and conduct for the young men of his day. But Leicester possessed neither courage nor capacity equal to the trust reposed in him; and his arbitrary and indolent conduct soon disgusted the people whom he was sent to assist. (Vandervynct.) They had, in the first impulse of their gratitude, given him the title of governor and captain-general of the provinces, in the hope of flattering Elizabeth. But this had a far contrary effect: she was equally displeased with the states and with Leicester; and it was with difficulty that, after many humble submissions, they were able to appease her. (Hume.)

To form a counterpoise to the power so lavishly conferred on Leicester, Prince Maurice was, according to the wise advice of Olden Barnevelt, raised to the dignity of *stadtholder*, captain-general, and admiral of Holland and Zealand. This is the first instance of these states taking on themselves the nomination to the dignity of *stadtholder*, for even William had held his commission from Philip, or in his name; but Friesland, Groningen, and Guelders had already appointed their local governors, under the same title, by the authority of the states-general, the archduke Mathias, or even of the provincial states. (Cerisier *Hist. Gen. des Provinces Unies,* t. iv.) Holland had now also at the head of its civil government a citizen full of talent and probity, who was thus able to contend with the insidious designs of Leicester against the liberty he nominally came to protect. This was Barnevelt, who was promoted from his office of pensionary of Rotterdam to that of Holland, and who accepted the dignity only on condition of being free to resign it if any accommodation of differences should take place with Spain. (Cerisier.)

Alexander of Parma had, by the death of his mother, in February, 1586, exchanged his title of prince for the superior one of Duke of Parma, and soon resumed his enterprises with his usual energy and success: various operations took place, in which the English on every opportunity distinguished themselves; particularly in an action near the town of Grave, in Brabant; and in the taking of Axel by escalade, under the orders of Sir Philip Sidney. A more important affair occurred near Zutphen, at a place called Warnsfeld, both which towns have given names to the action.

On this occasion the veteran Spaniards, under the Marquis of Guasto, were warmly attacked and completely defeated by the English; but the victory, was dearly purchased by the death of Sir Philip Sidney, who was mortally wounded in the thigh, and expired a few days afterwards, at the early age of 32 years. In addition to the valour, talent, and conduct, which had united to establish his fame, he displayed, on this last opportunity of his short career, an instance of humanity that sheds a new lustre on even a character like his. Stretched on the battlefield, in all the agony of his wound, and parched with thirst, his afflicted followers brought him some water, procured, with difficulty, at a distance, and during the heat of the fight. But Sidney, seeing a soldier lying near, mangled like himself, and apparently expiring, refused the water, saying, "Give it to that poor man; his sufferings are greater than mine." (Bor. xxi.)

Leicester's conduct was now become quite intolerable to the states. His incapacity and presumption were every day more evident and more revolting. He seemed to consider himself in a province wholly reduced to English authority, and paid no sort of attention to the very opposite character of the people. An eminent Dutch author accounts for this, in terms which may make an Englishman of this age not a little proud of the contrast which his character presents to what It was then considered. Grotius says, (Grot. *Ann.*):

> The Englishman, obeys like a slave, and governs like a tyrant; while the Belgian knows how to serve and to command with equal moderation.

The dislike between Leicester and those he insulted and misgoverned, soon became mutual. He retired to the town of Utrecht; and pushed his injurious conduct to such an extent, that he became an object of utter hatred to the provinces. All the friendly feelings towards England were gradually changed into suspicion and dislike. Conferences took place at The Hague between Leicester and the states, in which Barnevelt overwhelmed his contemptible shuffling by the force of irresistible eloquence and well-deserved reproaches; and after new acts of treachery, still more odious than his former, this unworthy favourite at last set out for England, to lay an account of his government at the feet of the queen. (Cerisier.)

The growing hatred against England was fomented by the true patriots, who aimed at the liberty of their country; and may be excused, from the various instances of treachery displayed, not only by the commander-in-chief, but by several of his inferiors in command. A strong fort, near Zutphen, under the government of Roland York, the town of Deventer, under that of William Stanly, and subsequently Guelders under a Scotchman named Fallot, were delivered up to the Spaniards by these men; and about the same time the English cavalry committed some excesses in Guelders and Holland, which added to the prevalent prejudice against the nation in general. (Bor. xx.) This enmity was no longer to be concealed. The partisans of Leicester, were one by one, under plausible pretexts, removed from the council of state; and Elizabeth having required from Holland the exportation into England of a large quantity of rye, it was firmly but respectfully refused, as inconsistent with the wants of the provinces.

Prince Maurice, from the caprice and jealousy of Leicester, now united in himself the whole power of command, and commenced that brilliant course of conduct, which consolidated the independence of his country, and elevated him to the first rank of military glory. His early efforts were turned to the suppression of the partiality which in some places existed for English domination; and he never allowed himself to be deceived by the hopes of peace held out by the emperor and the kings of Denmark and Poland. Without refusing their mediation, he laboured incessantly to organise every possible means for maintaining the war. His efforts were considerably favoured by the measures of Philip for the support of the league formed by the house of Guise against Henry III. and Henry IV. of France; but still more by the formidable enterprise which the Spanish monarch was now preparing against England.

Irritated and mortified by the assistance which Elizabeth had given to the revolted provinces, Philip resolved to employ his whole power in attempting the conquest of England itself; hoping afterwards to effect with ease the subjugation of the Netherlands. He caused to be built, in almost every port of Spain and Portugal, galleons, *carracks*, and other ships of war of the largest dimensions; and at the same time gave orders to the Duke of Parma to assemble in the harbours of Flanders as many vessels as he could collect together.

The Spanish fleet, consisting of more than 140 ships of the line, and manned by 20,000 sailors, assembled at Lisbon under the orders of the Duke of Medina Sidonia; while the Duke of Parma, uniting his forces, held himself ready on the coast of Flanders, with an army of 30,000 men, and 400 transports. This prodigious force obtained, in Spain, the ostentatious title of the Invincible Armada. Its destination was for a while attempted to be concealed, under pretext that it was meant for India, or for the annihilation of the United Provinces; but the mystery was soon discovered. At the end of May, the principal fleet sailed from the port of Lisbon; and being reinforced off Corunna by a considerable squadron, the whole armament steered its course for the shores of England.

The details of the progress and the failure of this celebrated attempt, are so thoroughly the province of English history, that they would be in this place superfluous. But it must not be forgotten, that the glory of the proud result was amply shared by the new republic, whose existence depended on it. While Howard and Drake held the British fleet in readiness to oppose the Spanish Armada, that of Holland, consisting of but twenty-five ships, under the command of Justin of Nassau, prepared to take a part in the conflict.

This gallant though illegitimate scion of the illustrious house whose name he upheld on many occasions, proved himself on the present worthy of such a father as William, and such a brother as Maurice. While the Duke of Medina Sidonia, ascending the channel as far as Dunkirk, there expected the junction of the Duke of Parma with his important reinforcement, Justin of Nassau, by a constant activity, and a display of intrepid talent, contrived to block up the whole expected force in the ports of Flanders from Lillo to Dunkirk.

The Duke of Parma found it impossible to force a passage on any one point; and was doomed to the mortification of knowing that the attempt was frustrated, and the whole force of Spain frittered away, discomfited, and disgraced, from the want of a co-operation, which he could not, however, reproach himself for having withheld. The issue of the memorable expedition, which cost Spain years of preparation, thousands of men, and millions of treasure, was received in the country which sent it forth with consternation and rage. Philip alone possessed or affected an apathy, which he covered with a veil of mock devotion that few were deceived by. At the news of the disaster, he fell on his knees, and rendering thanks for that gracious dispensation of Providence, expressed his joy that the calamity was not greater. (Hume.)

The people, the priests, and the commanders of the expedition were not so easily appeased, or so clever as their hypocritical master, in concealing their mortification. The priests accounted for this triumph of heresy as a punishment on Spain for suffering the existence of the *infidel* Moors in some parts of the country. (Strype, vol. iii.) The defeated admirals threw the whole blame on the Duke of Parma. He, on his part, sent an ample remonstrance to the king; and Philip declared that he was satisfied with the conduct of his nephew. Leicester died four days after the final defeat and dispersion of the armada. (Hume.)

The war in the Netherlands had been necessarily suffered to languish, while every eye was fixed on the progress of the armada, from formation to defeat. But new efforts were soon made by the Duke of

Parma to repair the time he had lost, and soothe, by his successes, the disappointed pride of Spain. Several officers now came into notice, remarkable for deeds of great gallantry and skill. None among those were so distinguished as Martin Schenck, a soldier of fortune, a man of ferocious activity, who began his career in the service of tyranny, and ended it by chance in that of independence. He changed sides several times; but no matter who he fought for, he did his duty well, from that unconquerable principle of pugnacity which seemed to make his sword a part of himself.

Schenck had lately, for the last time, gone over to the side of the states, and had caused a fort to be built in the isle of Betewe—that possessed of old by the Batavians—which was called by his name, and was considered the key to the passage of the Rhine. From this stronghold he constantly harassed the archbishop of Cologne, and had as his latest exploit surprised and taken the strong town of Bonn. While the Duke of Parma took prompt measures for the relief of the prelate, making himself master in the meantime of some places of strength, the indefatigable Schenck resolved to make an attempt on the important town of Nimeguen. He with great caution embarked a chosen body of troops on the Wahal, and arrived under the walls of Nimeguen at sunrise on the morning chosen for the attack.

His enterprise seemed almost crowned with success; when the inhabitants, recovering from their fright, precipitated themselves from the town; forced the assailants to retreat to their boats; and, carrying the combat into those overcharged and fragile vessels, upset several, and among others that which contained Schenck himself, who, covered with wounds, and fighting to the last gasp, was drowned with the greater part of his followers. His body, when recovered, was treated with the utmost indignity, quartered, and hung in portions over the different gates of the city. (D'Ewez.)

The following year was distinguished by another daring attempt on the part of the Hollanders, but followed by a different result. A captain named Haranguer concerted with one Adrien Vandenberg, a plan for the surprise of Breda, on the possession of which Prince Maurice had set a great value. The associates contrived to conceal in a boat, laden with turf (which formed the principal fuel of the inhabitants of that part of the country,) and of which Vandenberg was master, eighty determined soldiers, and succeeded in arriving close to the city without any suspicion being excited. One of the soldiers, named Matthew Helt, being suddenly affected with a violent cough, implored his comrades to put him to death, to avoid the risk of a discovery. But a corporal of the city guard having inspected the cargo with unsuspecting carelessness, the immolation of the brave soldier became unnecessary, and the boat was dragged into the basin by the assistance of some of the very garrison who were so soon to fall victims to the stratagem. At midnight the concealed soldiers quitted their hiding-places, leaped on shore, killed the sentinels, and easily became masters of the citadel. Prince Maurice, following close with his army, soon forced the town to submit, and put it into so good a state of defence, that count Mansfield, who was sent to retake it, was obliged to retreat after useless efforts to fulfil his mission.

The Duke of Parma, whose constitution was severely injured by the constant fatigues of war and the anxieties attending on the late transactions, had snatched a short interval for the purpose of recruiting his health at the waters of Spa. While at that place he received urgent orders from Philip to abandon for a while all his proceedings in the Netherlands, and to hasten into France with his whole disposable force, to assist the army of the League. The Battle of Yvri (in which the son of the unfortunate Count Egmont met his death while fighting in the service of his father's royal murderer) had raised the prospects and hopes of Henry IV. to a high pitch; and Paris, which he closely besieged, was on the point of yielding to his arms.

The Duke of Parma received his uncle's orders with great repugnance; and lamented the necessity of leaving the field of his former exploits open to the enterprise and talents of Prince Maurice. He nevertheless obeyed; and leaving Count Mansfield at the head of the government, he conducted his troops against the royal opponent, who alone seemed fully worthy of coping with him.

The attention of all Europe was now fixed on the exciting spectacle of a contest between these two greatest captains of the age. The glory of success, the fruit of consummate skill, was gained by Alexander; who, by an admirable manoeuvre, got possession of the town of Lagny-sur-Seine, under the very eyes of Henry and his whole army, and thus acquired the means of providing Paris with everything requisite for its defence. The French monarch saw all his projects baffled, and his hopes frustrated; while his antagonist, having fully completed his object, drew off his army through Champagne, and made a fine retreat through an enemy's country, harassed at every step, but with scarcely any loss.

But while this expedition added greatly to the renown of

the general, it considerably injured the cause of Spain in the Low Countries. Prince Maurice, taking prompt advantage of the absence of his great rival, had made himself master of several fortresses; and some Spanish regiments having mutinied against the commanders left behind by the duke of Parma, others, encouraged by the impunity they enjoyed, were ready on the slightest pretext to follow their example. Maurice did not lose a single opportunity of profiting by circumstances so favourable; and even after the return of Alexander he seized on Zutphen, Deventer, and Nimeguen, despite of all the efforts of the Spanish Army. The Duke of Parma, daily breaking down under the progress of disease, and agitated by these reverses, repaired again to Spa, taking at once every possible means for the recruitment of his army and the recovery of his health, on which its discipline and the chances of success now so evidently depended.

But all his plans were again frustrated by a renewal of Philip's peremptory orders to march once more into France, to uphold the failing cause of the League against the intrepidity and talent of Henry IV. At this juncture the Emperor Rodolf again offered his mediation between Spain and the United Provinces. But it was not likely that the confederated States, at the very moment when their cause began to triumph, and, their commerce was every day becoming more and more flourishing, would consent to make any compromise with the tyranny they were at length in a fair way of crushing.

The Duke of Parma again appeared in France in the beginning of the year 1592; and, having formed his communications with the army of the League, marched to the relief of the city of Rouen, at that period pressed to the last extremity by the Huguenot forces. After some sharp skirmishes—and one in particular, in which Henry IV. suffered his valour to lead him into a too rash exposure of his own and his army's safety—a series of manoeuvres took place, which displayed the talents of the rival generals in the most brilliant aspect.

Alexander at length succeeded in raising the siege of Rouen, and made himself master of Condebec, which commanded the navigation of the Seine. Henry, taking advantage of what appeared an irreparable fault on the part of the duke, invested his army in the hazardous position he had chosen; but while believing that he had the whole of his enemies in his power, he found that Alexander had passed the Seine with his entire force—raising his military renown to the utmost possible height, by a retreat which it was deemed utterly impossible to effect. (Browing, *Hist, of the Huguenots.*)

On his return to the Netherlands, the duke found himself again under the necessity of repairing to Spa, in search of some relief from the suffering, which was considerably increased by the effects of a wound received in this last campaign. In spite of his shattered constitution, he maintained to the latest moment the most active endeavours for the reorganisation of his army; and he was preparing for a new expedition into France, when, fortunately for the good cause in both countries, he was surprised by death on the 3rd of December, 1592, at the abbey of St.Vaast, near Arras, at the age of forty-seven years. As it was hard to imagine that Philip would suffer anyone who had excited his jealousy to die a natural death, that of the Duke of Parma was attributed to slow poison.

Alexander of Parma was certainly one of the most remarkable, and, it may be added, one of the greatest, characters of his day. Most historians have upheld him even higher perhaps than he should be placed on the scale; asserting that he can be reproached with very few of the vices of the age in which he lived. (Grotius.) Others consider this judgment too favourable, and accuse him of participation in all the crimes of Philip, whom he served so zealously. (Cerisier.) His having excited the jealousy of the tyrant, or even had he been put to death by his orders, would little influence the question; for Philip was quite capable of ingratitude or murder, to either an accomplice or an opponent of his baseness.

But even allowing that Alexander's one qualities were sullied by his complicity in these odious measures, we must, still in justice admit that they were too much in the spirit of the tunes, and particularly of the school in which he was trained; and while we lament that his political or private faults place him on so low a level, we must rank him as one of the very first masters in the art of war in his own or any other age.

CHAPTER 8

1592–1599

To the Independence of Belgium and the Death of Philip II.

The Duke of Parma had chosen the count of Mansfield for his successor, and the nomination was approved by the king. He entered on his government under most disheartening circumstances. The rapid conquests of Prince Maurice in Brabant and Flanders were scarcely less mortifying than the total disorganisation into which those two provinces had fallen. They were ravaged by bands of robbers called Picaroons, whose audacity reached such a height, that they opposed in large bodies the forces sent for their suppression by the government. They on one occasion killed the provost of Flanders, and burned his lieutenant in a hollow tree; and on another they mutilated a whole troop of the national militia, and their commander, with circumstances of most revolting cruelty. (D'Ewez.)

The authority of governor-general, though not the title, was now fully shared by the Count of Fuentes, who was sent to Brussels by the King of Spain; and the ill effects of this double viceroyalty was soon seen, in the brilliant progress of Prince Maurice, and the continual reverses sustained by the royalist armies. The king, still bent on projects of bigotry, sacrificed without scruple men and treasure for the overthrow of Henry IV. and the success of the League. The affairs of the Netherlands seemed now a secondary object; and he drew largely on his forces in that country for reinforcements to the ranks of his tottering allies. A final blow was, however, struck against the hopes of intolerance in France, and to the existence of the League, by the conversion of Henry IV. to the Catholic religion; he deeming theological disputes, which put the happiness of a whole kingdom in jeopardy, as quite subordinate to the public good. (Hume.)

Such was the prosperity of the United Provinces, that they had been enabled to send a large supply, both of money and men, to the aid of Henry, their constant and generous ally. And notwithstanding this, their armies and fleets, so far from suffering diminution, were augmented day by day. Philip, resolved to summon up all his energy for the revival of the war against the republic, now appointed the Archduke Ernest, brother of the Emperor Rodolf, to the post which the disunion of Mansfield and Fuentes rendered as embarrassing as it had become inglorious. This prince, of a gentle and conciliatory character, was received at Brussels with great magnificence and general joy; his presence reviving the deep-felt hopes of peace entertained by the suffering people. Such were also the cordial wishes of the prince (Bentivoglio); but more than one design, formed at this period against the life of Prince Maurice, frustrated every expectation of the kind.

A priest of the province of Namur, named Michael Renichon, disguised as a soldier, was the new instrument meant to strike another blow at the greatness of the house of Nassau, in the person of its gallant representative, Prince Maurice; as also in that of his brother, Frederic Henry, then ten years of age. On the confession of the intended assassin, he was employed by Count Berlaimont to murder the two princes, Renichon happily mismanaged the affair, and betrayed his intention. He was arrested at Breda, conducted to The Hague, and there tried and executed on the 3rd of June, 1594. (*Le Petit, liv.* 7.) This miserable wretch aroused the Archduke Ernest of having countenanced his attempt; but nothing whatever tends to criminate, while every probability acquits, that prince of such a participation.

In this same year a soldier named Peter Dufour embarked in a like atrocious plot. He, too, was seized and executed before he could carry it into effect; and to his dying hour, persisted in accusing the archduke of being his instigator. But neither the judges who tried, nor the best historians who record, his intended crime, gave any belief to this accusation. (Meteren.) The mild and honourable disposition of the prince held a sufficient guarantee against its likelihood; and it is not less pleasing to be able fully to join in the prevalent opinion, than to mark a spirit of candour and impartiality break forth through the mass of bad and violent passions which crowd the records of that age.

But all the esteem inspired by the personal character of Ernest could not overcome the repugnance of the United Provinces to trust to the apparent sincerity of the tyrant in whose name he made his overtures for peace. They were all respectfully and firmly rejected;

and Prince Maurice, in the meantime, with his usual activity, passed the Meuse and the Rhine, and invested and quickly took the town of Groningen, by which he consummated the establishment of the republic, and secured its rank among the principal powers of Europe. The Archduke Ernest, finding all his efforts for peace frustrated, and all hopes of gaining his object by hostility to be vain, became a prey to disappointment and regret, and died, from the effects of a slow fever, on the 21st of February, 1595; leaving to the Count of Fuentes the honours and anxieties of the government, subject to the ratification of the king.

This nobleman began the exercise of his temporary functions by an irruption into France, at the head of a small army; war having been declared against Spain by Henry IV., who, on his side, had dispatched the Admiral de Villars to attack Philip's possessions in Hainault and Artois. This gallant officer lost a battle and his life in the contest; and Fuentes, encouraged by the victory, took some frontier towns, and laid siege to Cambray, the great object of his plans. The citizens, who detested their governor, the Marquis of Bologni, who had for some time assumed an independent tyranny over them, gave up the place to the besiegers; and the citadel surrendered some days later. (Bentivoglio.)

After this exploit Fuentes returned to Brussels, where, notwithstanding his success, he was extremely unpopular, he had placed a part of his forces under the command of Mondragon, one of the oldest and cleverest officers in the service of Spain. Some trifling affairs took place in Brabant; but the arrival of the Archduke Albert, whom the king had appointed to succeed his brother Ernest in the office of governor-general, deprived Fuentes of any further opportunity of signalising his talents for supreme command. Albert arrived at Brussels. on the 11th of February, 1596, accompanied by the Prince of Orange, who, when Count of Beuren, had been carried off from the university of Louvain, twenty-eight years previously, and held captive in Spain during the whole of that period. (Meteren, *liv.* 18.)

The Archduke Albert, fifth son of the Emperor Maximilian II., and brother of Rodolf, stood high in the opinion of Philip his uncle, and merited his reputation for talents, bravery, and prudence. He had been early made archbishop of Toledo, and afterwards cardinal; but his profession was not that of these nominal dignities. He was a warrior and politician of considerate capacity; and had for some years faithfully served the king, as viceroy of Portugal. But Philip meant him for the more independent situation of sovereign of the Netherlands, and at the same time destined him to be the husband of his daughter Isabella. He now sent him, in the capacity of governor-general, to prepare the way for the important change; at once to gain the good graces of the people, and soothe, by this removal from Philip's too close neighbourhood, the jealousy of his son the hereditary prince of Spain. Albert brought with him to Brussels a small reinforcement for the army, with a large supply of money, more wanting at this conjuncture than men. He highly praised the conduct of Fuentes in the operations just finished; and resolved to continue the war on the same plan, but with forces much superior.

He opened his first campaign early; and, by a display of clever manoeuvring, which threatened an attempt to force the French to raise the siege of La Fére, in the heart of Picardy, he concealed his real design—the capture of Calais; and he succeeded in its completion almost before it was suspected. The Spanish and Walloon troops, led on by Rone, a distinguished officer, carried the first defences: after nine days of siege the place was forced to surrender; and in a few more the citadel followed the example. The archduke soon after took the towns of Ardres and Hulst; and by prudently avoiding a battle, to which he was constantly provoked by Henry IV., who commanded the French Army in person, he established his character for military talent of no ordinary degree.

He at the same time made overtures of reconciliation to the United Provinces, and hoped that the return of the Prince of Orange would be a means of effecting so desirable a purpose. But the Dutch were not to be deceived by the apparent sincerity of Spanish negotiation. They even doubted the sentiments of the Prince of Orange, whose attachments and principles had been formed in so hated a school; and nothing passed between them and him but mutual civilities. They clearly evinced their disapprobation of his intended visit to Holland; and he consequently fixed his residence in Brussels, passing his life in an inglorious neutrality.

A naval expedition formed in this year by the English and Dutch against Cadiz, commanded by the Earl of Essex, and Counts Louis and William of Nassau, cousins of Prince Maurice, was crowned with brilliant success, and somewhat consoled the provinces for the contemporary exploits of the archduke. (Hume.) But the following year opened with an affair, which at once proved his unceasing activity, and added largely to the reputation of his rival, Prince Maurice. The former had detached the Count of Varas, with about 6000 men, for the purpose of invading the province of Holland: but Maurice, with equal energy and superior talent, followed his movements; came up with him near Turnhout, on the 24th of January, 1597; and after a sharp action, of which the Dutch cavalry bore the whole brunt, Varas was killed, end his troops defeated with considerable loss.

******

This action may be taken as a fair sample of the difficulty with which any estimate can be formed of the relative losses on such occasions. The Dutch historians state the loss of the royalists, in killed, at upwards of 2000. Meteren, a good authority, says the peasants buried 2250; while Bentivoglio, an Italian writer in the interest of Spain, makes the number exactly half that amount. Grotius says that the loss of the Dutch was four men killed. Bentivoglio states it at 100. But, at either computation, it is clear that the affair was a brilliant one on the part of Prince Maurice.

******

This was in its consequences a most disastrous affair to the archduke. His army was disorganised, and his finances exhausted; while the confidence of the states in their troops and their general was considerably raised. But the taking of Amiens by Portocarrero, one of the most enterprising of the Spanish captains, gave a new turn to the failing fortunes of Albert. This gallant officer, whose greatness of mind, according to some historians, (Grotius, De Thou), was much disproportioned to the smallness of his person, gained possession of that important town by a well-conducted stratagem, and maintained his conquest valiantly till he was killed in its defence. Henry IV. made prodigious efforts to recover the place, the chief bulwark on that side of France; and having forced Montenegro, the worthy successor of Portocarrero, to capitulate, granted him and his garrison most honourable conditions. Henry, having secured Amiens against any new attack, returned to Paris, and made a triumphal entry into the city.

During this year Prince Maurice took a number of towns in rapid succession; and the states, according to their custom, caused various medals, in gold, silver, and copper, to be struck, to commemorate the victories which had signalised their arms. (D'Ewez.)

Philip II., feeling himself approaching the termination of his long and agitating career, now wholly occupied himself in negotiations for peace with France. Henry IV. desired it as anxiously. The pope, Clement VIII., encouraged by his exhortations this mutual inclination. The king of Poland sent ambassadors to The Hague and to London, to induce the states and Queen Elizabeth to become parties in a general pacification. These overtures led to no conclusion; but the conferences between France and Spain went on with apparent cordiality and great promptitude, and a peace was concluded between these powers at Vervins, on the 2nd of May, 1598.

Shortly after the publication of this treaty, another important act was made known to the world, by which Philip ceded to Albert and Isabella, on their being formally affianced—a ceremony which now took place—the sovereignty of Burgundy and the Netherlands. This act bears date the 6th of May, and was proclaimed with all the solemnity due to so important a transaction. It contained thirteen articles; and was based on the misfortunes which the absence of the sovereign had hitherto caused to the Low Countries. The Catholic religion was declared that of the state, in its full integrity. The provinces were guaranteed against dismemberment. The archdukes, by which title the joint sovereigns were designated without any distinction of sex, were secured in the possession, with right of succession to their children; and a provision was added, that in default of posterity their possessions should revert to the Spanish crown. (Grotius, *Hist. lib. viii.*)

The Infanta Isabella soon sent her procuration to the archduke, her affianced husband, giving him full power and authority to take possession of the ceded dominions in her name as in his own; and Albert was inaugurated with great pomp at Brussels, on the 22nd of August. Having put everything in order for the regulation of the government during his absence, he set out for Spain, for the purpose of accomplishing his spousals, and bringing back his bride to the chief seat of their joint power. But before his departure he wrote to the various states of the republic, and to Prince Maurice himself, strongly recommending submission and reconciliation. These letters received no answer; a new plot against the life of Prince Maurice, by a wretched individual named Peter Pann, having aroused the indignation of the country, and determined it to treat with suspicion and contempt every insidious proposition from the tyranny it defied. (D'Ewez.)

Albert placed his uncle, the Cardinal Andrew of Austria, at the head of the temporary government, and set out on his journey; taking the little town of Halle in his route, and deposing at the altar of the Virgin, who is there held in particular honour, his cardinal's hat as a token of his veneration. He had not made much progress when he received accounts of the demise of Philip II., who died, after long suffering, and with great resignation, on the 13th of September, 1596, at the age of seventy-two. (Watson.) Albert was several months on his journey through Germany; and the ceremonials of his union with the *infanta* did not take place till the 18th of April, 1599, when it was finally solemnised in the city of Valencia in Spain.

This transaction, by which the Netherlands were positively erected into a separate sovereignty, seems naturally to make the limits of another epoch in their history. It completely decided the division between the northern and southern provinces, which, although it had virtually taken place long previous to this period, could scarcely be considered as formally consummated until now. Here then we shall pause anew, and take a rapid review of the social state of the Netherlands during the last half century, which was beyond all doubt the most important period of their history, from the earliest times till the present.

It has been seen that when Charles V. resigned his throne and the possession of his vast dominions to his son, arts, commerce, and manufactures had risen to a state of considerable perfection throughout the Netherlands. The revolution, of which we have traced the rise and progress, naturally produced to those provinces which relapsed into slavery a most lamentable change in every branch of industry, and struck a blow at the genial prosperity, the effects of which are felt to this very day. Arts, science, and literature were sure to be checked and withered in the blaze of civil war; and we have now to mark the retrograde movements of most of those charms and advantages of civilized life, in which Flanders and the other southern states were so rich.

The rapid spread of enlightenment on religious subjects soon converted the manufactories and workshops of Flanders into so many conventicles of reform; and the clear-sighted artisans fled in thousands from the tyranny of Alva into England, Germany, and Holland—those happier countries, where the government adopted and went hand in hand with the progress of rational belief. Commerce followed the fate of manufactures. The foreign merchants one by one abandoned the theatre of bigotry and persecution; and even Antwerp, which had succeeded Bruges as the great mart of European traffic, was ruined by the horrible excesses of the Spanish soldiery, and never recovered from the shock. Its trade, its wealth, and its prosperity, were gradually transferred to Amsterdam, Rotterdam, and the towns of Holland

and Zealand; and the growth of Dutch commerce attained its proud maturity in the establishment of the India company in 1596, the effects of which we shall have hereafter more particularly to dwell on.

The exciting and romantic enterprises of the Portuguese and Spanish navigators in the fifteenth and sixteenth centuries, roused all the ardour of other nations for those distant adventures; and the people of the Netherlands were early influenced by the general spirit of Europe. If they were not the discoverers of new worlds, they were certainly the first to make the name of European respected and venerated by the natives.

Animated by the ardour which springs from the spirit of freedom and the enthusiasm of success, the United Provinces laboured for the discovery of new outlets for their commerce and navigation. The government encouraged the speculations of individuals, which promised fresh and fertile sources of revenue, so necessary for the maintenance of the war. (Grotius, *Hist. viii.*) Until the year 1581 the merchants of Holland and Zealand were satisfied to find the productions of India at Lisbon, which was the mark of that branch of trade ever since the Portuguese discovered the passage by the Cape of Good Hope. But Philip II., having conquered Portugal, excluded the United Provinces from the ports of that country; and their enterprising mariners were from that period driven to those efforts which rapidly led to private fortune and general prosperity. The English had opened the way in this career; and the states-general having offered a large reward for the discovery of a north-west passage, frequent and most adventurous voyages took place. Houtman, Le Maire, Heemskirk, Ryp, and others, became celebrated for their enterprise, and some for their perilous and interesting adventures.

The United Provinces were soon without any rival on the seas. In Europe alone they had 1200 merchant-ships in activity, and upwards of 70,000 sailors constantly employed. (Grot. iv.) They built annually 2000 vessels. In the year 1598, eighty ships sailed from their ports for the Indies or America. They carried on, besides, an extensive trade on the coast of Guinea, whence they brought large quantities of gold-dust; and found, in short, in all quarters of the globe the reward of their skill, industry, and courage.

The spirit of conquest soon became grafted on the habits of trade. Expedition succeeded to expedition. Failure taught wisdom to those who did not want bravery. The random efforts of individuals were succeeded by organised plans, under associations well constituted and wealthy; and these soon gave birth to those eastern and western companies before alluded to. The disputes between the English and the Hanseatic towns were carefully observed by the Dutch, and turned to their own advantage. The English manufacturers, who quickly began to flourish, from the influx of Flemish workmen under the encouragement of Elizabeth, formed companies in the Netherlands, and sent their cloths into those very towns of Germany which formerly possessed the exclusive privilege of their manufacture. (Meteren, *liv*. 19.) These towns naturally felt dissatisfied, and their complaints were encouraged by the king of Spain. The English adventurers received orders to quit the empire; and, invited by the states-general, many of them fixed their residence in Middleburg, which became the most celebrated woollen market in Europe.

The establishment of the Jews in the towns of the republic forms a remarkable epoch in the annals of trade. This people, so outraged by the lothesome bigotry which Christians have not blushed to call religion, so far from being depressed by the general persecution, seemed to find it a fresh stimulus to the exertion of their industry. To escape death in Spain, and Portugal they took refuge in Holland, where toleration encouraged, and just principles of state maintained them. They were at first taken for Catholics, and subjected to suspicion; but when their real faith was understood, they were no longer molested.

Astronomy and geography, two sciences so closely allied with and so essential to navigation, flourished now throughout Europe. Ortilius of Antwerp, and Gerard Mercator of Rupelmonde, were two of the greatest geographers of the sixteenth century; and the reform in the calendar at the end of that period gave stability to the calculations of time, which had previously suffered all the inconvenient fluctuations attendant on the old style.

Literature had assumed during the revolution in the Netherlands the almost exclusive and repulsive aspect of controversial learning. The university of Douay, installed in 1562 as a new screen against the piercing light of reform, quickly became the strong-hold of intolerance. That of Leyden, established by the efforts of the Prince of Orange, soon after the famous siege of that town in 1574, was on a less exclusive plan—its professors being in the first instance drawn from Germany. (De Smet.) Many Flemish historians succeeded in this century to the ancient and uncultivated chroniclers of preceding times; the civil wars drawing forth many writers, who recorded what they witnessed, but often in a spirit of partisanship and want of candour, which seriously embarrasses him who desires to learn the truth on both sides of an important question. Poetry declined and drooped in these times of tumult and suffering; and the chambers of rhetoric, to which its cultivation had been chiefly due, gradually lost their influence, and finally ceased to exist.

In fixing our attention on the republic of the United Provinces during the epoch now completed, we feel the desire, and lament the impossibility, of entering on the details of government in that most remarkable state. For these we must refer to what appears to us the best authority for clear and ample information on the prerogative of the *stadtholder*, the constitution of the states-general, the privileges of the tribunals and local assemblies, and other points of moment concerning the principles of the Belgic confederation. (See Cerisier, *Hist. Gen. des Prov. Unies, t. iv.*)

CHAPTER 9

1599–1604

TO THE CAMPAIGN OF PRINCE MAURICE AND SPINOLA.

Previous to his departure for Spain, the Archduke Albert had placed the government of the provinces which acknowledged his domination in the hands of his uncle, the Cardinal Andrew of Austria, leaving in command of the army Francisco Mendoza, Admiral of Aragon. The troops at his disposal amounted to 22,000 fighting men—a formidable force, and enough to justify the serious apprehensions of the republic. Albert, whose finances were exhausted by payments made to the numerous Spanish and Italian mutineers, had left orders with Mendoza to secure some place on the Rhine, which might open a passage for free quarters in the enemy's country.

But this unprincipled officer forced his way into the neutral districts of Cleves and Westphalia; and with a body of executioners ready to hang up all who might resist, and of priests to prepare them for death, he carried such terror on his march that no opposition was ventured. (Reid, *xv.*) The atrocious cruelties of Mendoza and his troops baffle all description: on one occasion they murdered, in cold blood, the Count of Walkenstein, who surrendered his castle on the express condition of his freedom; and they committed every possible excess that may be imagined of ferocious soldiery encouraged by a base commander. (Meteren, *liv. xxi.*)

Prince Maurice soon put into motion, to oppose this army of brigands, his small disposable force of about 7000 men. With these, however, and a succession of masterly manoeuvres, he contrived to preserve the republic from invasion, and to paralyze and almost destroy an army three times superior in numbers to his own. (Cerisier.) The horrors committed by the Spaniards, in the midst of peace, and without the slightest provocation, could not fail to excite the utmost indignation in a nation so fond of liberty and so proud as Germany. The Duchy of Cleves felt particularly aggrieved; and Sybilla, the sister of the duke, a real heroine in a glorious cause, so worked on the excited passions of the people by her eloquence and her tears, that she persuaded all the orders of the state to unite against the odious enemy. Some troops were suddenly raised; and a league was formed between several princes of the empire to revenge the common cause. The Count de la Lippe was chosen general of their united forces; and the choice could not have fallen on one more certainly incapable, or more probably treacherous. (Cerisier.)

The German Army, with their usual want of activity, did not open the campaign till the month of June. It consisted of 14,000 men; and never was an army so badly conducted. (De Thou, *liv.* 122.) Without money, artillery, provisions, or discipline, it was at any moment ready to break up and abandon its incompetent general: and on the very first encounter with the enemy, and after a loss of a couple of hundred men, it became self-disbanded; and, flying in every direction, not a single man could be rallied to clear away this disgrace.

The states-general, cruelly disappointed at this result of measures, from which they had looked for so important a diversion in their favour, now resolved on a vigorous exertion of their own energies, and determined to undertake a naval expedition of a magnitude greater than any they had hitherto attempted. The force of public opinion was at this period more powerful than it had ever yet been in the United Provinces: for a great number of the inhabitants, who, during the life of Philip II., conscientiously believed that they could not lawfully abjure the authority once recognised and sworn to, became now liberated from those respectable although absurd scruples; and the death of one unfeeling despot gave thousands of new citizens to the state.

A fleet of seventy-three vessels, carrying 8000 men, was soon equipped, under the order of Admiral Vander Goes; and after a series of attempts on the coasts of Spain, Portugal, Africa, and the Canary Isles, this expedition, from which the most splendid results were expected, was shattered, dispersed, and reduced to nothing, by a succession of unheard-of mishaps.

To these disappointments were now added domestic dissensions in the republic, in consequence of the new taxes absolutely necessary for the exigencies of the state. The conduct of Queen Elizabeth greatly added to the general embarrassment: she called for the payment of her former loans; insisted on the recall of the English troops; and declared her resolution to make peace with Spain. (Cerisier.) Several German princes promised aid in men and money, but never furnished either; and in this most critical juncture, Henry IV. was the only foreign sovereign who did not abandon the republic. He sent them 1000 Swiss troops, whom he had in his pay; allowed them to levy 3000 more in France; and gave them a loan of 200,000 crowns—a very convenient supply in their exhausted state.

The Archdukes Albert and Isabella arrived in the Netherlands in September, and made their entrance into Brussels with unexampled magnificence. They soon found themselves in a situation quite as critical as was that of the United Provinces, and both parties displayed immense energy to remedy their mutual embarrassments. The winter was extremely rigorous; so much so, as to allow of military operations being undertaken on the ice. Prince Maurice soon commenced a Christmas campaign by taking the town of Wachtendenck; and he followed up his success by obtaining possession of the important forts of Crevecoeur and St Andrew, in the island of Bommel. A most dangerous mutiny at the same time broke out in the army of the archdukes; and Albert seemed left without troops or money, at the very beginning of his sovereignty.

But these successes of Prince Maurice were only the prelude to an expedition of infinitely more moment, arranged with the utmost secrecy, and executed with an energy scarcely to be looked for from the situation of the states. This was nothing less than an invasion poured into the very heart of Flanders, thus putting the archdukes on the defence of their own most vital possessions, and changing completely the whole character of the war. (Grot. viii.) The whole disposable troops of the republic, amounting to about 17,000 men, were secretly assembled in the island of Walcheren, in the month of June; and setting sail for Flanders, they disembarked near Ghent, and arrived on the 20th of that month under the walls of Bruges. Some previous negotiations with that town had led the prince to expect that it would have opened its gates at his approach. In this he was, however, disappointed; and after taking possession of some forts in the neighbourhood, he continued his march to Nieuport, which place he invested on the 1st of July.

At the news of this invasion the archdukes, though taken by surprise, displayed a promptness and decision that proved them worthy of the sovereignty which seemed at stake. With incredible activity they mustered, in a few days, an army of 12,000 men, which they passed in review near Ghent. On this occasion Isabella, proving her title to a place among those heroic women with whom the age abounded, rode through the royalist ranks, and harangued them in a style of inspiring eloquence that inflamed their courage and secured their fidelity. Albert, seizing the moment of this excitement, put himself at their head, and marched to seek the enemy, leaving his intrepid wife at Bruges, the nearest town to the scene of the action he was resolved on.

He gained possession of all the forts taken and garrisoned by Maurice a few days before; and pushing forward with his apparently irresistible troops, he came up on the morning of the 2nd of July with a large body of those of the states, consisting of about 3000 men, sent forward under the command of Count Ernest of Nassau to reconnoitre and judge of the extent of this most unexpected movement: for Prince Maurice was, in his turn, completely surprised; and not merely by one of those manoeuvres of war by which the best generals are sometimes deceived, but by an exertion of political vigour and capacity of which history offers few more striking examples.

Such a circumstance, however, served only to draw forth a fresh display of those uncommon talents, which in so many various accidents of war had placed Maurice on the highest rank for military talent. The detachment under Count Ernest of Nassau was chiefly composed of Scottish infantry; and this small force stood firmly opposed to the impetuous attack of the whole royalist army—thus giving time to the main body under the prince to take up a position, and form in order of battle. Count Ernest was at length driven back, with the loss of 800 men killed, almost all Scottish; and being cut off from the rest of the army, was forced to take refuge in Ostend, which town was in possession of the troops of the states.

The army of Albert now marched on, flushed with this first success and confident of final victory. Prince Maurice received them with the courage of a gallant soldier and the precaution of a consummate general. He had caused the fleet of ships of war and transports, which had sailed along the coast from Zealand, and landed supplies of ammunition and provisions, to retire far from the shore, so as to leave to his army no chance of escape but in victory. The commissioners from the states, who always accompanied the prince as a council of observation rather than of war, had retired to Ostend in great consternation, to wait the issue of the battle which now seemed inevitable. A scene of deep feeling and heroism was the next episode of this memorable day, and throws the charm of natural affection over those circumstances in which glory too seldom leaves a place for the softer emotions of the heart.

When the patriot army was in its position, and firmly waiting the advance of the foe, Prince Maurice turned to his brother, Frederick Henry, then sixteen years of age, and several young noblemen, English, French, and German, who like him attended on the great captain to learn the art of war: he pointed out in a few words the perilous situation in which he was placed; declared his resolution to conquer or perish on the battlefield; and recommended the boyish band to retire to Ostend, and wait for some less desperate occasion, to share his renown or revenge his fall. Frederick Henry spurned the affectionate suggestion, and swore to stand by his brother to the last; and all his young companions adopted the same generous resolution.

The army of the states was placed in order of battle, about a league in front of Nieuport, in the sand-hills with which the neighbourhood abounds, its left wing resting on the seashore. Its losses of the morning, and of the garrison left in the forts near Bruges, reduced it to an almost exact equality with that of the archduke. Each of these armies was composed of that variety of troops which made them respectively an epitome of the various nations of Europe. The patriot force contained Dutch, English, French, German, and Swiss, under the orders of Count Louis of Nassau, Sir Francis and Sir Horace Vere, brothers and English officers of great celebrity, with other distinguished captains.

The archduke mustered Spaniards, Italians, Walloons and Irish in his ranks, led on by Mendoza, La Berlotta and their fellow-veterans. Both armies were in the highest state of discipline, trained to war by long service, and enthusiastic in the several causes which they served; the two highest principles of enthusiasm urging them on—religious fanaticism on the one hand, and the love of freedom on the other. The rival generals rode along their respective lines; addressed a few brief sentences of encouragement to their men, and presently the bloody contest began.

It was three o'clock in the afternoon when the archduke commenced the attack. His advanced guard, commanded by Mendoza and composed of those former mutineers who now resolved to atone for their misconduct, marched across the sand-hills with desperate resolution. They soon came into contact with the English contingent under Francis Vere, who was desperately wounded in the shock. The assault was almost irresistible. The English, borne down by numbers, were forced to give way; but the main body pressed on to their support. Horace Vere stepped forward to supply his brother's place. Not an inch of ground more was gained or lost, the firing ceased, and pikes and swords crossed each other in the resolute conflict of man to man. The action became general along the whole line. The two commanders-in-chief were at all points. Nothing could exceed their mutual display of skill and courage. At length the Spanish cavalry, broken by the well-directed fire of the patriot artillery, fell back on the infantry and threw it into confusion.

The archduke at the same instant was wounded by a lance in the cheek, unhorsed, and forced to quit the field. The report of his death, and the sight of his war-steed galloping alone across the field, spread alarm through the royalist ranks. Prince Maurice saw and seized on the critical moment. He who had so patiently maintained his position for three hours of desperate conflict, now knew the crisis for a prompt and general advance. He gave the word and led on to the charge, and the victory was at once his own. (Bentivoglio, Vandervynct, &c.)

The defeat of the royalist army was complete. The whole of the artillery, baggage, standards, and ammunition, fell into the possession of the conquerors. Night coming on saved those who fled, and the nature of the ground prevented the cavalry from consummating the destruction of the whole. As for as the conflicting accounts of the various historians may be compared and calculated on, the royalists had 3000 killed, and among them several officers of rank; while the patriot army, including those who fell in the morning action, lost somethings more than half the number. The archduke, furnished with a fresh horse, gained Bruges in safety; but he only waited there long enough to join his heroic wife, with whom he proceeded rapidly to Ghent, and thence to Brussels. Mendoza was wounded and taken prisoner, and with difficulty saved by Prince Maurice from the fury of the German auxiliaries.

The morale effects produced by this victory on the vanquishers and vanquished, and on the state of public opinion throughout Europe, was immense; but its immediate consequences were incredibly trifling. Not one result in a military point of view followed an event which appeared almost decisive of the war. Nieuport was again invested three days after the battle; but a strong reinforcement entering the place saved it from all danger, and Maurice found himself forced for want of supplies to abandon the scene of his greatest exploit. He returned to Holland, welcomed by the acclamations of his grateful country, and exciting the jealousy and hatred of all who envied his glory or feared his power. Among the sincere and conscientious republicans who saw danger to the public liberty in the growing influence of a successful soldier, placed at the head of affairs and endeared to the people by every hereditary and personal claim, was Olden Barneveldt the pensionary; and from this period may be traced the growth of the mutual antipathy which led to the sacrifice of the most virtuous statesman of Holland, and the eternal disgrace of its hitherto heroic chief.

The states of the Catholic provinces assembled at Brussels now gave the archdukes to understand that nothing but peace could satisfy their wishes or save the country from exhaustion and ruin. Albert saw the reasonableness of their remonstrances, and attempted to carry the great object into effect. The states-general listened to his proposals. Commissioners were appointed on both sides to treat of terms. They met at Bergen-op-Zoom; but their conferences were broken up almost as soon as commenced. The Spanish deputies insisted on the submission of the republic to its ancient masters. Such a proposal was worse than insulting: it proved the inveterate insincerity of those with whom it originated, and who knew it could not be entertained for a moment Preparations for hostilities were therefore commenced on both sides, and the whole of the winter was thus employed.

Early in the spring Prince Maurice opened the campaign at the head of 16,000 men, chiefly composed of English and French, who seemed throughout the contest to forget their national animosities, and to know no rivalry but that of emulation in the cause of liberty. The town of Rhinberg soon fell into the hands of the prince. His next attempt was against Bois-le-duc; and the siege of this place was signalised by an event that flavoured of the chivalric contests now going out of fashion. A Norman gentleman of the name of Bréauté, in the service of Prince Maurice, challenged the royalist garrison to meet him and twenty of his comrades in arms under the walls of the place.

The cartel was accepted by a Fleming named Abramzoom, but better known by the epithet *Leckerbeetje* (savoury bit,) who, with twenty more, met Bréauté and his friends. The combat was desperate. The Flemish champion was killed at the first shock by his Norman challenger: but the latter falling into the hands of the enemy, they treacherously and cruelly put him to death, in violation of the strict conditions of the fight Prince Maurice was forced to raise the siege of Bois-le-duc, and turn his attention in another direction. (D'Ewez.)

The Archduke Albert had now resolved to invest Ostend, a place of great importance to the United Provinces, but little worth to either party in comparison with the dreadful waste of treasure and human life which was the consequence of its memorable siege. Sir Francis Vere commanded in the place at the period of its final investment; but governors, garrisons, and besieging forces, were renewed and replaced with a rapidity which gives one of the most frightful instances of the ravages of war.

The siege of Ostend lasted upwards of three years. It became a school for the young nobility of all Europe, who repaired to either one or the other party to learn the principles and the practice of attack and defence. Everything that the art of strategy could devise was resorted to on either side. The slaughter in the various assaults, sorties, and bombardments, was enormous. Squadrons at sea gave a double interest to the land operations; and the celebrated brothers Frederick and Ambrose Spinola founded their reputation on these opposing elements.

Frederick was killed in one of the naval combats with the Dutch galleys, and the fame of reducing Ostend was reserved for Ambrose. This afterwards celebrated general had undertaken the command at the earnest entreaties of the archduke and the King of Spain, and by the firmness and vigour of his measures he revived the courage of the worn-out assailants of the place. Redoubled attacks and multiplied mines at length reduced the town to a mere mass of ruin, and scarcely left its still undaunted garrison sufficient footing on which to prolong their desperate defence.

Ostend at length surrendered, on the 23rd of September, 1604, and the victors marched in over its crumbled walls and shattered batteries. Scarcely a vestige of the place remained beyond those terrible evidences of destruction. Its ditches filled up with the rubbish of ramparts, bastions, and redoubts, left no distinct line of separation between the operations of its attack and its defence. It resembled lather a vast sepulchre than a ruined town, a mountain of earth and rubbish, without a single house in which the wretched remnant of the inhabitants could hide their heads—a monument of desolation on which victory might have sat and wept.

During the progress of this memorable siege Queen Elizabeth of England had died, after a long and, it must be pronounced, a glorious reign; though the glory belongs rather to the nation than to the monarch, whose memoir is marked with indelible stains of private cruelty, as in the cases of Essex and Mary Queen of Scots, and of public wrongs, as in that of her whole system of tyranny in Ireland. With respect to the United Provinces she was a harsh protectress and a capricious ally. She in turns advised them to remain faithful to the old impurities of religion and to their intolerable king; refused to incorporate them with her own states; and then used her best efforts for subjecting them to her sway. She seemed to take pleasure in the uncertainty to which she reduced them, by constant demands for payment of her loans, and threats of making peace with Spain.

Thus the states-general were not much affected by the news of her death: and so rejoiced were they at the accession of James I. to the throne of England, that all the bells of Holland rang out merry peals; bonfires were set blazing all over the country; a letter of congratulation was dispatched to the new monarch; and it was speedily followed by a solemn embassy, composed of Prince Frederick Henry, the Grand Pensionary De Barneveldt, and others of the first dignitaries of the republic. (Cerisier, vol. iv.) These ambassadors were grievously disappointed at the reception given to them by James, who treated them as little better than rebels to their lawful king. But this first disposition to contempt and insult was soon overcome by the united talents of Barneveldt and the great Duke of Sully, who were at the same period ambassadors from France at the English court.

The result of the negotiations was an agreement between these two powers to take the republic under their protection, and use their best efforts for obtaining the recognition of its independence by Spain. (Hume, vol. iv.) The states-general considered themselves amply recompensed for the loss of Ostend, by the taking of Ecluse, Rhynberg, and Grave, all of which had in the interval surrendered to Prince Maurice; but they were seriously alarmed on finding themselves abandoned by King James, who concluded a separate peace with Philip III. of Spain in the month of August this year. (Meteren.)

This event gives rise to a question very important to the honour of James, and consequently to England itself, as the acts of the absolute monarchs of those days must be considered as those of the nations which submitted to such a form of government. Historians of great authority, (Hume, vol. vi.) have asserted that it appeared that, by a secret agreement, the king had expressly reserved the power of sending assistance to Holland. Others deny the existence of this secret article; and lean heavily on the reputation of James for his conduct in the transaction. (Cerisier, t. iv.) It must be considered a very doubtful point, and is to be judged rather by subsequent events than by any direct testimony.

The two monarchs stipulated in the treaty that "neither was to give support of any kind to the revolted subjects of the other." It is nevertheless true that James did not withdraw his troops from the service of the states; but he authorised the Spaniards to levy soldiers in England. The United Provinces were at once afflicted and indignant at this equivocal conduct Their first impulse was to deprive the English of the liberty of navigating the Scheldt. They even arrested the progress of several of their merchant-ships. But soon after, gratified at finding that James received their deputy with the title of ambassador, they resolved to dissimulate their resentment

Prince Maurice and Spinola now took the field with their respective armies; and a rapid series of operations placing them in direct contact, displayed their talents in the most striking points of view. The first steps on the part of the prince were a new invasion of Flanders, and an attempt on Antwerp, which he hoped to carry before the Spanish Army could arrive to its succour. But the promptitude and sagacity of Spinola defeated this plan, which Maurice was obliged to abandon after some loss; while the royalist general resolved to signalise himself by some important movement, and, ere his design was suspected, he had penetrated into the province of Overyssel, and thus retorted his rival's favourite measure of carrying the war into the enemy's country. Several towns were rapidly reduced; but Maurice flew towards the threatened provinces, and by his active measures forced Spinola to fall back on the Rhine and take up a position near Roeroord, (Grotius, *lib.* xiv.) where he was impetuously attacked by the Dutch Army.

But the cavalry having followed up too slowly the orders of Maurice, his hope of surprising the royalists was frustrated; and the Spanish forces, gaining time by this hesitation, soon changed the fortune of the day. The Dutch cavalry shamefully took to flight, despite the gallant endeavours of both Maurice and his brother Frederick Henry; and at this juncture a large reinforcement of Spaniards arrived under the command of Velasco. Maurice now brought forward some companies of English and French infantry under Horatio Vere and D'Omerville, also a distinguished officer. The battle was again fiercely renewed; and the Spaniards now gave way, and had been completely defeated, had not Spinola put in practice an old and generally successful stratagem. He caused almost all the drums of his army to beat in one direction, so as to give the impression that a still larger reinforcement was approaching.

Maurice, apprehensive that the former panic might find a parallel in a fresh one, prudently ordered a retreat, which he was able to effect in good order, in preference to risking the total disorganisation of his troops. The loss on each side was nearly the same; but the glory of this hard-fought day remained on the side of Spinola, who proved himself a worthy successor of the great Duke of Parma, and an antagonist with whom Maurice might contend without dishonour. (Grotius, *Hist. lib.* xiv.)

The naval transactions of this year restored the balance which Spinola's successes had begun to turn in favour of the royalist cause. A squadron of ships, commanded by Hautain Admiral of Zealand, attacked a superior force of Spanish vessels close to Dover, and defeated them with considerable loss. But the victory was sullied by an act of great barbarity. All the soldiers found on board the captured ships were tied two and two, and mercilessly flung into the sea. Some contrived to extricate themselves, and gained the shore by swimming; others were picked up by the English boats, whose crews witnessed the scene and hastened to their relief. The generous British seamen could not remain neuter in such a moment, nor repress their indignation against those whom they had hitherto so long considered as friends. The Dutch vessels pursuing those of Spain which fled into Dover harbour, were fired on by the cannon of the castle and forced to give up the chase.

The English loudly complained that the Dutch had on this occasion violated their territory; and this transaction laid the foundation of the quarrel which subsequently broke out between England and the republic, and which the jealousies of rival merchants in either state unceasingly fomented. In this year also, the Dutch succeeded in capturing the chief of the Dunkirk privateers, which had so long annoyed their trade; and they cruelly ordered sixty of the prisoners to be put to death. But the people, more humane than the authorities, rescued them from the executioners and set them free. (Cerisier.)

But these domestic instances of success and inhumanity, were trifling, in comparison with the splendid train of distant events, accompanied by a course of wholesale benevolence that redeemed the traits of petty guilt. The maritime enterprises of Holland, forced by the imprudent policy of Spain to seek a wider career than in the. narrow seas of Europe, were day by day extended in the Indies. To ruin if possible, their increasing trade, Philip III. sent out the Admiral Hurtado, with a fleet of eight galleons and thirty-two galleys. The

Dutch squadron of five vessels, commanded by Wolfert Hermanszoon, attacked them off the coast of Malabar, and his temerity was crowned with great success. He took two of their vessels, and completely drove the remainder from the Indian seas. He then concluded a treaty with the natives of the isle of Banda, by which he promised to support them against the Spaniards and Portuguese, on condition that they were to give his fellow-countrymen the exclusive privilege of purchasing the spices of the island. This treaty was the foundation of the influence which the Dutch so soon succeeded in forming in the East Indies; and they established it by a candid, mild, and tolerant conduct, strongly contrasted with the pride and bigotry which had signalised every act of the Portuguese and Spaniards.

The prodigious success of the Indian trade occasioned numerous societies to be formed all through the republic. But by their great number they became at length injurious to each other. The spirit of speculation was pushed too far; and the merchants, who paid enormous prices for India goods, found themselves forced to sell in Europe at a loss. Many of those societies were too weak, in miitary force as well as in capital, to resist the armed competition of the Spaniards, and to support themselves in their disputes with the native princes. At length the states-general resolved to unite the whole of these scattered partnerships into one grand company, which was soon organised on a solid basis, that led erelong to incredible wealth at home, and a rapid succession of conquests in the East. (Richesse de la Hollande, t. i.)

CHAPTER 10

1606–1619

The states-general now resolved to confine their military operations to a war merely defensive. Spinola had, by his conduct during the late campaign, completely revived the spirits of the Spanish troops, and excited at least the caution of the Dutch. He now threatened the United Provinces with invasion; and he exerted his utmost efforts to raise the supplies necessary for the execution of his plan. He not only exhausted the resources of the King of Spain and the archduke, but obtained money on his private account from all those usurers who were tempted by his confident anticipations of conquest. He soon equipped two armies of about 12,000 men each. At the head of one of those he took the field; the other, commanded by the Count of Bucquoi, was destined to join him in the neighbourhood of Utrecht; and he was then resolved to push forward with the whole united force into the very heart of the republic.

Prince Maurice in the meantime concentrated his army, amounting to 12,000 men, and prepared to make head against his formidable opponents. By a succession of the most prudent manoeuvres he contrived to keep Spinola in check, disconcerted all his projects, and forced him to content himself with the capture of two or three towns—comparatively insignificant conquest. Desiring to wipe away the disgrace of this discomfiture, and to risk everything for the accomplishment of his grand design, Spinola used every method to provoke the prince to a battle, even though a serious mutiny among his troops, and the impossibility of forming a junction with Bucquoi, had reduced his force below that of Maurice; but the latter, to the surprise of all who expected a decisive blow, retreated from before the

Italian general—abandoning the town of Groll, which immediately fell into Spinola's power, and giving rise to manifold conjectures and infinite discontent at conduct so little in unison with his wonted enterprise and skill. Even Henry IV. acknowledged it did not answer the expectation he had formed from Maurice's splendid talents for war. (Sully's Mem. t. iii.) The fact seems to be, that the prince, much as he valued victory, dreaded peace more; and that he was resolved to avoid a decisive blow, which, in putting an end to the contest, would at the same time have decreased the individual influence in the state, which his ambition now urged him to augment by every possible means.

The Dutch naval expeditions this year were not more brilliant than those on land. Admiral Hautain, with twenty ships, was surprised off Cape St Vincent by the Spanish fleet. The formidable appearance of their galleons inspired on this occasion a perfect panic among the Dutch sailors. They hoisted their sails and fled, with the exception of one ship, commanded by Vice-Admiral Klaazoon, whose desperate conduct saved the national honour. Having held out until his vessel was quite unmanageable, and almost his whole crew killed or wounded, he prevailed on the rest to agree to the resolution he had formed, knelt down on the deck, and putting up a brief prayer for pardon for the act, thrust a light into the powder-magazine, and was instantly blown up with his companions. Only two men were snatched from the sea by the Spaniards; and even these, dreadfully burnt and mangled, died in the utterance of curses on the enemy. (Cerisier.)

This disastrous occurrence was soon, however, forgotten in the rejoicings for a brilliant victory gained the following year by Heemskirk, so celebrated for his voyage to Nova Zembla, and by his conduct in the East. He set sail from the ports of Holland in the month of March, determined to signalise himself by some great exploit, now necessary to redeem the disgrace which had begun to sully the reputation of the Dutch Navy. He soon got intelligence that the Spanish fleet lay at anchor in the bay of Gibraltar, and he speedily prepared to offer them battle. Before the combat began, he held a council of war, and addressed the officers in an energetic speech, in which he displayed the imperative call on their valour to conquer or die in the approaching conflict. He led on to the action in his own ship; and, to the astonishment of both fleets, he bore right down against the enormous galleon in which the flag of the Spanish admiral in chief was hoisted.

D'Avila could scarcely believe the evidence of his eyes at this audacity: he at first burst into laughter at the notion; but as Heemskirk approached, he cut his cables and attempted to escape under the shelter of the town. The heroic Dutchman pursued him through the whole of the Spanish fleet, and soon forced him to action. At the second broadside Heemskirk had his left leg carried off by a cannonball, and he almost instantly died, exhorting his crew to seek for consolation in the defeat of the enemy. Verhoef, the captain of the ship, concealed the admiral's death; and the whole fleet continued the action with a valour worthy the spirit in which it was commenced. The victory was soon decided: four of the Spanish galleons were sunk or burned, the remainder fled; and the citizens of Cadiz trembled with the apprehension of sack and pillage. But the death of Heemskirk, when made known to the surviving victors, seemed completely to paralyze them: they attempted nothing further; but sailing back to Holland with the body of their lamented chief, thus paid a greater tribute to his importance than was to be found in the mausoleum erected to his memory in the city of Amsterdam. (Vandervynct.)

The news of this battle reaching Brussels before it was known in Holland, contributed not a little to quicken the anxiety of the archdukes for peace. The king of Spain, worn out by the war which drained his treasury, had for some time ardently desired it. The Portuguese made loud complaints of the ruin that threatened their trade and their East Indian colonies. (Grotius.) The Spanish ministers were fatigued with the apparently interminable contest which baffled all their calculations. (Bentivoglio.) Spinola, even in the midst of his brilliant career, found himself so overwhelmed with debts, and so oppressed by the reproaches of the numerous creditors who were ruined by his default of payment, that he joined in the general demand for repose. (Cerisier.) In the month of May, 1607, proposals were made by the archdukes, in compliance with the general desire; and their two plenipotentiaries, Van Wittenhorst and Gevaerts, repaired to The Hague.

Public opinion in the United States was divided on this important question. An instinctive hatred against the Spaniards, and long habits of warfare, influenced the great mass of the people to consider any overture for peace as some wily artifice aimed at their religion and liberty. War seemed to open inexhaustible sources of wealth; while peace seemed to threaten the extinction of the courage, which was now as much a habit as war appeared to be a want. This reasoning was particularly convincing to Prince Maurice, whose fame, with a large portion of his authority and revenues, depended on the continuance of hostilities: it was also strongly relished and supported in Zealand generally, and in the chief towns, which dreaded the rivalry of Antwerp. But those who bore the burden of the war saw the subject under a different aspect (Bentivoglio): they feared that the present state of things would lead to their conquest by the enemy, or to the ruin of their liberty by the growing power of Maurice. They hoped that peace would consolidate the republic and cause the reduction of the debt, which now amounted to 26,000,000 florins. At the head of the party who so reasoned was De Barneveldt; and his name is a guarantee with posterity for the wisdom of the opinion.

To allow the violent opposition to subside, and to prevent any explosion of party feuds, the prudent Barneveldt suggested a mere suspension of arms, during which the permanent interests of both states might be calmly discussed: he even undertook to obtain Maurice's consent to the armistice. The prince listened to his arguments, and was apparently convinced by them. He, at any rate, sanctioned the proposal; but he afterwards complained that Barneveldt had deceived him, in representing the negotiation as a feint for the purpose of persuading the kings of France and England to give greater aid to the republic. (Cerisier.) It is more than likely that Maurice reckoned on the improbability of Spain's consenting to the terms of the proposed treaty; and, on that chance, withdrew an opposition which could scarcely be ascribed to any but motives of personal ambition.

It is, however, certain that his discontent at this transaction, either with himself or Barneveldt, laid the foundation of that bitter enmity which proved fatal to the life of the latter, and covered his own name, otherwise glorious, with undying reproach.

The United Provinces positively refused to admit even the commencement of a negotiation without the absolute recognition of their independence by the archdukes. A new ambassador was accordingly chosen on the part of these sovereigns, and empowered to concede this important admission. This person attracted considerable attention, from his well-known qualities as an able diplomatist. He was a monk of the order of St Francis, named John de Neyen, a native of Antwerp, and a person as well versed in court intrigue as in the studies of the cloister. He, in the first instance, repaired secretly to The Hague; and had several private interviews with Prince Maurice and Barneveldt, before he was regularly introduced to the states-general in his official character.

Two different journeys were undertaken by this agent between The Hague and Brussels, before he could succeed in obtaining a perfect understanding as to the specific views of the archdukes. The suspicions of the states-general seem fully justified by the dubious tone of the various communications, which avoided the direct admission of the required preliminary as to the independence of the United Provinces. It was at length concluded in explicit terms; and a suspension of arms for eight months was the immediate consequence.

But the negotiation for peace was on the point of being completely broken, in consequence of the conduct of Neyen, who justified every doubt of his sincerity by an attempt to corrupt Aarsens the *greffier* (clerk) of the states-general, or at least to influence his conduct in the progress of the treaty. Neyen presented him, in the name of the archdukes, and as a token this esteem, with a diamond of great value and a bond for 50,000 crowns. Aarsens accepted these presents with the approbation of Prince Maurice, to whom he had confided the circumstance, and who was no doubt delighted at what promised a rupture to the negotiations.

Verreiken, a counsellor of state, who assisted Neyen in his diplomatic labours, was formally summoned before the assembled states-general, and there Barneveldt handed to him the diamond and the bond; and at the same time read him a lecture of true republican severity on the subject Verreiken was overwhelmed by the violent attack: he denied the authority of Neyen for the measure he had taken; and remarked that "it was not surprising that monks, naturally interested and avaricious, judged others by themselves." (Jeannin, vol. i.) This repudiation of Neyen's suspicious conduct, seems to have satisfied the stern resentment of Barneveldt, and the party which so earnestly laboured for peace. In spite of all the opposition of Maurice and his partisans, the negotiation went on.

In the month of January, 1608, the various ambassadors were assembled at The Hague. Spinola was the chief of the plenipotentiaries appointed by the King of Spain; and Jeannin, president of the parliament of Dijon, a man of rare endowments, represented France. Prince Maurice, accompanied by his brother Frederick Henry, the various Counts of Nassau his cousins, and a numerous escort, advanced some distance to meet Spinola, conveyed him to The Hague in his own carriage, and lavished on him all the attentions reciprocally due between two such renowned captains during the suspension of their rivalry. The president Richardst was, with Neyen and Verreiken, ambassador from the archdukes; but Barneveldt, (Vandervynct), and Jeannin appear to have played the chief parts in the important transaction which now filled all Europe with anxiety. Every state was more or less concerned in the result; and the three great monarchies of England, France, and Spain, had all a vital interest at stake. The conferences were therefore frequent; and the debates assumed a great variety of aspects, which long kept the civilized world in suspense.

King James was extremely jealous of the more prominent part taken by the French ambassadors, and of the subaltern consideration held by his own envoys, Winwood and Spencer, in consequence of the disfavour in which he himself was held by the Dutch people. It appears evident that, whether deservedly or the contrary, England was at this period unpopular in the United Provinces, while France was looked up to with the greatest enthusiasm. This is not surprising, when we compare the characters of Henry IV. and James I., bearing in mind how much of national reputation at the time depended on the personal conduct of kings; and how political situations influence, if they do not create, the virtues and vices of a people. Independent of the suspicions of his being altogether unfavourable to the declaration required by the United Provinces from Spain, to which James's conduct had given rise, he had established some exactions which greatly embarrassed their fishing expeditions on the coasts of England.

The main points for discussion, and on which depended the decision for peace or war, were those which concerned religion; and the demand, on the part of Spain, that the United Provinces should renounce all claims to the navigation of the Indian seas. (Vandervynct.) Philip required for the Catholics of the United Provinces the free exercise of their religion; this was opposed by the states-general: and the archduke Albert, seeing the impossibility of carrying that point, dispatched his confessor Fra Inigo de Briznella, to Spain. This Dominican was furnished with the written opinion of several theologians, that the king might conscientiously slur over the article of religion; and he was the more successful with Philip, as the Duke of Lerma, his prime minister, was resolved to accomplish the peace at any price. (Vandervynct.)

The conferences at The Hague were therefore not interrupted on this question; but they went on slowly, months being consumed in discussions on articles, of trifling importance. They were, however, resumed in the month of August with greater vigour. It was announced that the King of Spain abandoned the question respecting religion; but that it was in the certainty that his moderation would be recompensed by ample concessions on that of the Indian trade, on which he was inexorable. This article became the rock on which the whole negotiation eventually split. The court of Spain, on the one hand, and the states-general on the other, inflexibly maintained their opposing claims. It was in vain that the ambassadors turned and twisted the subject with all the subtleties of diplomacy. Every possible expedient was used to shake the determination of the Dutch.

But the influence of the East India company, the islands of Zealand, and the city of Amsterdam, prevailed over all. Reports of the avowal on the part of the King of Spain, that he would never renounce his title to the sovereignty of the United Provinces, unless they abandoned the Indian navigation, and granted the free exercise of religion, threw the whole diplomatic corps into confusion; and on the 25th of August, the states-general announced to the Marquis of Spinola and the other ambassadors, that the congress was dissolved, and that all hopes of peace were abandoned. (Grotius, *lib. xvii.*)

Nothing seemed now likely to prevent the immediate renewal of hostilities, when the ambassadors of France and England proposed the mediation of their respective masters for the conclusion of a truce for several years. The King of Spain and the archdukes were well satisfied to obtain even this temporary cessation of the war; but Prince Maurice and a portion of the Provinces strenuously opposed the proposition. The French and English ambassadors, however, in concert with Barneveldt, who steadily maintained his influence, laboured incessantly to overcome those difficulties; and finally succeeded in overpowering all opposition to the truce. A new congress was agreed on, to assemble at Antwerp for the consideration of the conditions; and the states-general agreed to remove from The Hague to Bergen-op-Zoom, to be more within reach, and ready to co-operate in the negotiation.

But, before matters assumed this favourable turn, discussions and disputes had intervened on several occasions to render fruitless every effort of those who so incessantly laboured for the great causes of humanity and the general good. On one occasion, Barneveldt, disgusted with the opposition of Prince Maurice and his partisans, had actually resigned his employments; but brought back by the solicitations of the states-general, and reconciled to Maurice by the intervention of Jeannin, the negotiations for the truce were resumed; and, under the auspices of the ambassadors, they were happily terminated. After two years' delay, this long wished for truce was concluded, and signed on the 9th of April, 1609, to continue for the space of twelve years.

(Jeannin. Grotius. Bentivoglio. Vandervynct.)

This celebrated treaty contained thirty-two articles; and its fulfilment on either side was guaranteed by the kings of France and England. Notwithstanding the time taken up in previous discussions, the treaty is one of the most vague and unspecific state papers that exist. The archdukes, in their own names and in that of the King of Spain, declared the United Provinces to be free and independent states, on which they renounced all claim whatever. By the third article each party was to hold respectively the places which they possessed at the commencement of the armistice. The fourth and fifth articles grant to the republic, but in a phraseology obscure and even doubtful, the right of navigation and free trade to the Indies. The eighth contains all that regards the exercise of religion; and the remaining clauses are wholly relative to points of internal trade, custom-house regulations and matters of private interest. (Vandervynct.)

Ephemeral and temporary as this peace appeared, it was received with almost universal demonstrations of joy by the population of the Netherlands in their two grand divisions. Everyone seemed to turn towards the enjoyment of tranquillity with the animated composure of tired labourers looking forward to a day of rest and sunshine. This truce brought a calm of comparative happiness upon the country, which an almost unremitting tempest had desolated for nearly half a century; and, after so long a series of calamity, all the national advantages of social life seemed about to settle on the land.

The attitude which the United Provinces assumed at this period was indeed a proud one. They were not now compelled to look abroad and solicit other states to become their masters. They had forced their old tyrants to acknowledge their independence; to come and ask for peace on their own ground; and to treat with them on terms of no doubtful equality. They had already become so flourishing, so powerful, and so envied, that they who had so lately excited but compassion from the neighbouring states were now regarded with such jealousy as rivals, unequivocally equal, may justly inspire in each other.

The ten southern provinces, now confirmed under the sovereignty of the house of Austria, and from this period generally distinguished by the name of Belgium, immediately began, like the northern division of the country, to labour for the great object of repairing the dreadful sufferings caused by their long, and cruel war. Their success was considerable. Albert and Isabella, their sovereigns, joined to considerable probity of character and talents for government, a fund of humanity which led them to unceasing acts of benevolence. The whole of their dominions quickly began to recover from the ravages of war. Agriculture and the minor operations of trade resumed all their wonted activity. But the manufactures of Flanders were no more; and the grander exercise of commerce seemed finally removed to Amsterdam and the other chief towns of Holland. (Vandervynct.)

This tranquil course of prosperity in the Belgian provinces was only once interrupted during the whole continuance of the twelve years' truce, and that was in the year following its commencement. The death of the Duke of Cleves and Juliers, in this year, gave rise to serious disputes for the succession to his states, which was claimed by several of the princes of Germany. The elector of Brandenburg and the Duke of Neubourg were seconded both by France and the United Provinces; and a joint army of both nations, commanded by Prince Maurice and the Marshal de la Châtre, was marched into the county of Cleves. (Meteren.) After taking possession of the town of Juliers, the allies retired, leaving the two princes above mentioned in a partnership possession of the disputed states.

But this joint sovereignty did not satisfy the ambition of either, and serious divisions arose between them, each endeavouring to strengthen himself by foreign alliances. The archdukes Albert and Isabella were drawn into the quarrel; and they dispatched Spinola at the head of 20,000 men to support the Duke of Neubourg, whose pretensions they countenanced. Prince Maurice, with a Dutch Army, advanced on the other hand to uphold the claims of the elector of Brandenburg. Both generals took possession of several towns; and this double expedition offered the singular spectacle of two opposing armies, acting in different interests, making conquests, and dividing an important inheritance, without the occurrence of one act of hostility to each other. (Bentivoglio, *Relazione del Card.*) But the interference of the court of Madrid had nearly been the cause of a new rupture. The greatest alarm was excited in the Belgic provinces; and nothing but the prudence of the archdukes and the forbearance of the states-general could have succeeded in averting the threatened evil.

With the exception of this bloodless mimicry of war, the United Provinces presented for the space of twelve yean a long-continued picture of peace, as the term is generally received; but a peace so disfigured by intestine troubles, and so stained by actions of despotic cruelty, that the period which should have been that of its greatest happiness becomes but an example of its worst disgrace.

The assassination of Henry IV., in the year 1609, was a new instance of the bigoted atrocity which reigned paramount in Europe at the time; and whilst robbing France of one of its best monarchs, it deprived the United Provinces of their truest and most powerful friend. Henry has, from his own days to the present, found a ready eulogy in all who value kings in proportion as they are distinguished by heroism, without ceasing to evince the feelings of humanity. Henry seems to have gone as far as man can go, to combine wisdom, dimity, and courage, with all those endearing qualities of private life which alone give men a prominent hold upon the sympathies of their kind. We acknowledge his errors, his faults, his follies, only to love him the better. We admire his valour and generosity, without being shocked by cruelty or disgusted by profusion. We look on his greatness without envy; and in tracing his whole career we seem to walk hand in hand, beside a dear companion, rather than to follow the footsteps of a mighty monarch.

But the death of this powerful supporter of their efforts for freedom, and the chief guarantee for its continuance, was a trifling calamity to the United Provinces, in comparison with the rapid fall from the true point of glory so painfully exhibited in the conduct of their own domestic champion. It had been well for Prince Maurice of Nassau that the last shot fired by the defeated Spaniards in the battle of Nieuport had struck him dead in the moment of his greatest victory, and on the summit of his fame. From that celebrated day he had performed no deed of war that could raise his reputation as a soldier, and all his acts as *stadtholder* were calculated to sink him below the level of civil virtue and just government. His two campaigns against Spinola had redounded more to the credit of his rival than to his own; and his whole conduct during the negotiation for the truce too plainly betrayed the unworthy nature of his ambition, founded on despotic principles.

It was his misfortune to have been completely thrown out of the career for which he had been designed by nature and education. War was his element. By his genius, he improved it as a science: by his valour, he was one of those who raised it from the degradation of a trade to the dignity of a passion. But when removed from the camp to the council-room, he became all at once a common man. His frankness degenerated into roughness; his decision into despotism; his courage into cruelty. He gave a new proof of the melancholy fact, that circumstances may transform the most apparent qualities of virtue into those opposite vices between which human wisdom is baffled when it attempts to draw a decided and invariable line.

Opposed to Maurice in almost every one of his acts was, as we have already seen, Barneveldt, one of the truest patriots of any time or country; and, with the exception of William the great Prince of Orange, the most eminent citizen to whom the affairs of the Netherlands have given celebrity. A hundred pens have laboured to do honour to this truly virtuous man. (Aubery, *Mem.* Cerisier, &c.) His greatness has found a record in every act of his life; and his death, like that of William, though differently accomplished, was equally a martyrdom for the liberties of his country. We cannot enter minutely into the train of circumstances which for several years brought Maurice and Barneveldt into perpetual concussion with each other. Long after the completion of the truce, which the latter so mainly aided in accomplishing, every minor point in the domestic affairs of the republic seemed merged in the conflict between the *stadtholder* and the pensionary.

Without attempting to specify these, we may say generally, that almost every one redounded to the disgrace of the prince and the honour of the patriot. But the main question of agitation was the fierce dispute which soon broke out between two professors of theology of the university of Leyden, Francis Gomar and James Arminius. We do not regret on this occasion that our confined limits spare us the task of recording in detail controversies on points of speculative doctrine far beyond the reach of the human understanding, and therefore presumptuous, and the decision of which cannot be regarded as of vital importance by those who justly estimate the grand principles of Christianity. The whole strength of the intellects which had long been engaged in the conflict for national and religious liberty, was now directed to metaphysical theology, and wasted upon interminable disputes about predestination and grace. Barneveldt enrolled himself among the partisans of Arminius; Maurice became a Gomarist

It was, however, scarcely to be wondered at, that a country so recently delivered from slavery both in church and state should run into wild excesses of intolerance, before sectarian principles were thoroughly understood and definitively fixed. Persecutions of various kinds were indulged in against Papists, Anabaptists, Socinians, and all the shades of doctrine into which Christianity had split. Every minister who, in the milder spirit of Lutheranism, strove to moderate the rage of Calvinistic enthusiasm, was openly denounced by its partisans; and one, named Gaspard Koolhaas, was actually excommunicated by a synod, and denounced in plain terms to the devil. (Brandt. *Hist, du Reform.*) Arminius had been appointed professor at Leyden in 1603, for the mildness of his doctrines, which were joined to most affable manners, a happy temper, and a purity of conduct which no calumny could successfully traduce. (Bayle, art. Arminius.)

His colleague Gomar, a native of Bruges, learned, violent, and rigid in sectarian points, soon became jealous of the more popular professor's influence. A furious attack on the latter was answered by recrimination; and the whole battery of theological authorities was reciprocally discharged by one or other of the disputants. The states-general interfered between them: they were summoned to appear before the council of state; and grave politicians listened for hours to the dispute. Arminius obtained the advantage, by the apparent reasonableness of his creed, and the gentleness and moderation of his conduct. He was meek, while Gomar was furious; and many of the listeners declared that they would rather die with the charity of the former than in the faith of the latter. A second hearing was allowed them before the states of Holland. Again, Arminius took the lead; and the controversy went on unceasingly, till this amiable man, worn out by his exertions and the presentiment of the evil which these disputes were engendering for his country, expired in his 49th year, piously persisting in his opinions. (Bert. *Orat. Funeb.*)

The Gomarists now loudly called for a national synod, to regulate the points of faith. The Arminians remonstrated on various grounds, and thus acquired the name of *Remonstrants*, by which they were soon generally distinguished. The most deplorable contests ensued. Serious riots occurred in several of the towns of Holland; and James I. of England could not resist the temptation of entering the polemical lists, as a champion of orthodoxy and a decided Gomarist. His hostility was chiefly directed against Vorstius, the successor and disciple of Arminius. He pretty strongly recommended to the states-general to have him burned for heresy. (*King James's Works.*) His inveterate intolerance knew no bounds; and it completed the melancholy picture of absurdity which the whole affair presents to reasonable minds. (See James's letter to the states-general; Mercure Francais, t. xi.)

In this dispute, which occupied and agitated all, it was impossible that Barneveldt should not choose the congenial temperance and toleration of Arminius. Maurice, with probably no distinct conviction, or much interest in the abstract differences on either side, joined the Gomarists. (Cerisier, t. v.) His motives were purely temporal; for the party he espoused was now decidedly as much political as religious. King James rewarded him by conferring on him the riband of the order of the Garter, vacant by the death of Henry IV. of France. (Rapin, *lib. xviii.*) The ceremony of investment was performed with great pomp by the English ambassador at The Hague; and James and Maurice entered from that time into a closer and more uninterrupted correspondence than before. (Lauriers de Nassau.)

During the long continuance of the theological disputes, the United Provinces had nevertheless made rapid strides towards commercial greatness; and the year 1616 witnessed the completion of an affair which was considered the consolidation of their independence. This important matter was the recovery of the towns of Brille and Flessingue, and the fort of Rammekins, which had been placed in the hands of the English as security for the loan granted to the republic by Queen Elizabeth. The whole merit of the transaction was due to the perseverance and address of Barneveldt acting on the weakness and the embarrassments of King James. Religious contention did not so fully occupy Barneveldt, but that he kept a constant eye on political concerns. He was well informed on all that passed in the English court: he knew the wants of James, and was aware of his efforts to bring about the marriage of his son with the *infanta* of Spain.

The danger of such an alliance was evident to the penetrating Barneveldt, who saw in perspective the probability of the wily Spaniard's obtaining from the English monarch possession of the strong places in question. He therefore resolved on obtaining their recovery; and his great care was to get them back with a considerable abatement of the enormous debt for which they stood pledged, and which now amounted to 8,000,000 florins. (Cerisier.)

Barneveldt commenced his operations by sounding the needy monarch through the medium of Noel Caron, the ambassador from the states-general; and he next managed so as that James himself should offer to give up the towns, thereby allowing a fair pretext to the states for claiming a diminution of the debt. The English garrisons were unpaid; and their complaints brought down a strong remonstrance from James, and excuses from the states, founded on the poverty of their financial resources. The negotiation rapidly went on, in the same spirit of avidity on the part of the king, and of good management on that of his debtors. It was finally agreed that the states should pay in full of the demand 2,728,000 florins (about 250,000*l.* sterling,) being about one-third of the debt. Prince Maurice repaired to the cautionary towns in the month of June, and received them at the hands of the English governors; the garrisons at the same time entering into the service of the republic. (Carleton's *Mem.* vol. i. Hume, vol. viii.)

The accomplishment of this measure afforded the highest satisfaction to the United States. It caused infinite discontent in England; and James, with the common injustice of men who make a bad bargain, (even though its conditions be of their own seeking, and suited to their own convenience,) turned his own self-dissatisfaction into bitter hatred against him whose watchful integrity had successfully laboured for his country's good. Barneveldt's leaning towards France and the Arminians filled the measure of James's unworthy enmity. (Cabala, i.) Its effects were soon apparent, on the arrival at The Hague of Carleton, who succeeded Winwood as James's ambassador. The haughty pretensions of this diplomatist, whose attention seemed turned to theological disputes rather than politics, gave great disgust; and he contributed not a little to the persecution which led to the tragical end of Barneveldt's valuable life. (Cerisier, t. v.)

While this indefatigable patriot was busy in relieving his country from its dependence on England, his enemies accused him of the wish to reduce it once more to Spanish tyranny. Francis Aarsens, son to him who proved himself so incorruptible when attempted to be bribed by Neyen, was one of the foremost of the faction who now laboured for the downfall of the pensionary. He was a man of infinite dissimulation; versed in all the intrigues of courts; and so deep in all their tortuous tactics, that cardinal Richelieu, well qualified to prize that species of talent, declared that he knew only three great political geniuses, of whom Francis Aarsens was one. (Cerisier.)

Prince Maurice now almost openly avowed his pretensions to absolute sovereignty: he knew that his success wholly depended on the consent of Barneveldt. To seduce him to favour his designs, he had recourse to the dowager Princess of Orange, his mother-in-law, whose gentle character and exemplary conduct had procured her universal esteem, and the influence naturally attendant on it. Maurice took care to make her understand that her interest in his object was not trifling. Long time attached to Gertrude van Mechlen, his favourite mistress, who had borne him several children, he now announced his positive resolution to remain unmarried; so that his brother Frederick Henry, the dowager's only son, would be sure to succeed to the sovereignty he aimed at.

The princess, not insensible to this appeal, followed the instructions of Maurice, and broached the affair to Barneveldt; but he was inexorable. He clearly explained to her the perilous career on which the prince proposed to enter. He showed how great, how independent, how almost absolute, he might continue, without shocking the principles of republicanism by grasping at an empty dignity, which could not virtually increase his authority, and would most probably convulse the state to its foundation, and lead to his own ruin. The princess, convinced by his reasoning, repaired to Maurice; but instead of finding him as ready a convert as she herself had been, she received as cold an answer as was compatible with a passionate temper, wounded pride, and disappointed ambition. The princess and Barneveldt recounted the whole affair to Maurier the French ambassador; and his son has transmitted it to posterity. (Aubery du Maurier's *Memoirs*.)

We cannot follow the misguided prince in all the winding ways of intrigue and subterfuge through which he laboured to reach his object. Religion, the holiest of sentiments, and Christianity, the most sacred of its forms, were perpetually degraded by being made the pretexts for that unworthy object. He was for a while diverted from its direct pursuit by the preparation made to afford assistance to some of the allies of the republic. Fifty thousand florins a month were granted to the Duke of Savoy, who was at war with Spain, (Carleton, vol. i.) and 7000 men, with nearly forty ships, were dispatched to the aid of the republic of Venice, in its contest with Ferdinand Archduke of Gratz, who was afterwards elected emperor.

The honorary empire of the seas seems at this time to have been successfully claimed by the United Provinces: they paid back with interest the haughty conduct with which they had been long treated by the English (Carleton's *Mem.* vol. i.); and they refused to pay the fishery duties to which the inhabitants of Great Britain were subject. The Dutch sailors had even the temerity, under pretext of pursuing pirates, to violate the British territory: they set fire to the town of Crookhaven, in Ireland, and massacred several of the inhabitants. King James, immersed in theological studies, appears to have passed slightly over this outrage. (Carleton's *Mem.* vol. i.) More was to have been expected from his usual attention to the affairs of Ireland; his management of which ill-fated country is the best feature of his political character, and ought, to Irish feelings at least, to be considered to redeem its many errors.

But he took fire at the news that the states had prohibited the importation of cloth dyed and dressed in England. It required the best exertion of Barneveldt's talents to pacify him; and it was not easy to effect this through the jaundiced medium of the Ambassador Carleton. But it was unanswerably argued by the pensionary, that the manufacture of cloth was one of those ancient and natural sources of wealth which England had ravished from the Netherlands, and which the latter was justified in recovering by every effort consistent with national honour and fair principles of government. (Carleton.)

The influence of Prince Maurice had gained complete success for the Calvinist party, in its various titles of Gomarists, non-remonstrants, &c. The audacity and violence of these ferocious sectarians knew no bounds. Outrages, too many to enumerate, became common through the country; and Arminianism was on all sides assailed and persecuted. Barneveldt frequently appealed to Maurice without effect; and all the efforts of the former to obtain justice by means of the civil authorities were paralyzed by the inaction in which the prince retained the military force. In this juncture, the magistrates of various towns, spurred on by Barneveldt, called out the national militia, termed *Waardegelders*, which possessed the right of arming at its own expense for the protection of the public peace.

Schism upon schism was the consequence, and the whole country was reduced to that state of anarchy so favourable to the designs of an ambitious soldier already in the enjoyment of almost absolute power. Maurice possessed all the hardihood and vigour suited to such an occasion. At the head of two companies of infantry, and accompanied by his brother Frederick Henry, he suddenly set out at night from The Hague; arrived at the Brille; and in defiance of the remonstrances of the magistrates, and in violation of the rights of the town, he placed his devoted garrison in that important place. (Grot. *Apol.*) To justify this measure, reports were spread that Barneveldt intended to deliver it up to the Spaniards; and the ignorant, insensate, and ungrateful people swallowed the calumny. (Cerisier.)

This and such minor efforts were, however, all subservient to the one grand object of utterly destroying, by a public proscription, the whole of the patriot party, now identified with Arminianism. A national synod was loudly clamoured for by the Gomarists; and in spite of all opposition on constitutional grounds, it was finally proclaimed. Uitenbogaard, the enlightened pastor and friend of Maurice, who on all occasions laboured for the general good, now moderated, as much as possible, the violence of either party: but he could not persuade Barneveldt to render himself, by compliance, a tacit accomplice with a measure that he conceived fraught with violence to the public privileges. He had an inflexible enemy in Carleton the English ambassador. His interference carried the question; and it was at his suggestion that Dordrecht, or Dort, was chosen for the assembling of the synod. (Carleton's *Mem.*Vol. i.) Du Manner, the French ambassador, acted on all occasions as a mediator (Aubery, *Mem.* art. Maurier); but to obtain influence at such a time it was necessary to become a partisan. Several towns—Leyden, Gouda, Rotterdam, and some others—made a last effort for their liberties, and formed a fruitless confederation.

Barneveldt solicited the acceptance of his resignation of all his offices. The states-general implored him not to abandon the country at such a critical moment: he consequently maintained his post. Libels the most vindictive and atrocious were published and circulated against him; and at last, forced from his silence by these multiplied calumnies, he put forward his "Apology," addressed to the States of Holland.

This dignified vindication only produced new outrages; Maurice, now become Prince of Orange by the death of his elder brother without children, employed his whole authority to carry his object, and crush Barneveldt. At the head of his troops he seized on towns, displaced magistrates, trampled underfoot all the ancient privileges of the citizens, and openly announced his intention to overthrow the federative constitution. (Cerisier. t. v.) His bold conduct completely terrified the states-general. They thanked him; they consented to disband the militia; formally invited foreign powers to favour and protect the synod about to be held at Port. The return of Carleton from England, where he had gone to receive the more positive promises of support from King James, was only wanting, to decide Maurice to take the final step (Uitenbog. *Hist.*); and no sooner did the ambassador arrive at The Hague, than Barneveldt and his most able friends, Grotius, Hoogerbeets, and Ledenberg, were arrested in the name of the states-general. (Cerisier.)

The country was taken by surprise: no resistance was offered. The concluding scenes of the tragedy were hurried on: violence was succeeded by violence, against public feeling and public justice. Maurice became completely absolute in everything but in name. The supplications of ambassadors, the protests of individuals, the arguments of statesmen, were alike unavailing to stop the torrent of despotism and injustice. The synod of Dort was opened on the 13th of November, 1618. Theology was mystified; religion disgraced; Christianity outraged. And after 152 sittings, during six months' display of ferocity and fraud, the solemn mockery was closed on the 9th of May, 1619, by the declaration of its president, that "its miraculous labours had made hell tremble." (Brandt, t. ii.) Proscriptions, banishments, and death, were the natural consequences of this synod.

The divisions which it had professed to extinguish were rendered a thousand times more violent than before. Its decrees did incalculable ill to the cause they were meant to promote. The Anglican church was the first to reject the canons of Dort with horror and contempt. (Cerisier.) The Protestants of France and Germany, and even Geneva, the nurse and guardian of Calvinism, were shocked and disgusted, and unanimously softened down the rigor of their respective creeds. But the moral effects of this memorable conclave were too remote to prevent the sacrifice which almost immediately followed the celebration of its rites. A trial by twenty-four prejudiced enemies, by courtesy called judges, which in its progress and its result throws judicial dignity into scorn, ended in the condemnation of Barneveldt and his fellow patriots, for treason against the liberties they had vainly laboured to save. Barneveldt died on the scaffold by the hands of the executioner, on the 13th of May, 1619, in the 72nd year of his age. Grotius and Hoogerbeets were sentenced to perpetual imprisonment. Ledenberg committed suicide in his cell, sooner than brave the tortures which he anticipated at the hands of his enemies.

Many more pages than we are able to afford sentences, might be devoted to the details of these iniquitous proceedings, and an account of their awful consummation. The pious heroism of Barneveldt was never excelled by any martyr to the most holy cause. He appealed to Maurice against the unjust sentence which condemned him to death; but he scorned to beg his life. He met his fate with such temperate courage as was to be expected from the dignified energy of his life. His last words were worthy a philosopher whose thoughts, even in his latest moments, were superior to mere personal hope or fear, and turned to the deep mysteries of his being. "O God!" cried De Barneveldt, "what then is man?" as he bent his head to the sword that severed it from his body, and sent the inquiring spirit to learn the great mystery for which it longed.

CHAPTER 11

1619–1625

TO THE DEATH OF PRINCE MAURICE.

The Princess-Dowager of Orange, and Du Maurier the French ambassador, had vainly implored mercy for the innocent victim at the hands of the inexorable *stadtholder*. Maurice refused to see his mother-in-law: he left the ambassador's appeal unanswered. This is enough for the rigid justice of history, that cannot be blinded by partiality, but hands over to shame, at the close of their career, even those whom she nursed in the very cradle of heroism. But an accusation has become current, more fatal to the fame of Prince Maurice, because it strikes at the root of his claims to feeling, which could not be impugned by a mere perseverance in severity that might have sprung from mistaken views. It is asserted, but only as general belief, that he witnessed the execution of Barneveldt. (Grotius, Aubery, &c.)

The little window of an octagonal tower, overlooking the square of the Binnenhof at The Hague, where the tragedy was acted, is still shown as the spot from which the prince gazed on the scene. Almost concealed from view among the clustering buildings of the place, it is well adapted to give weight to the tradition; but it may not, perhaps, even now be too late to raise a generous incredulity as to an assertion of which no eye-witness attestation is recorded, and which might have been the invention of malignity. There are many statements of history which it is immaterial to substantiate or disprove.

Splendid fictions of public virtue have often produced their good, if once received as fact; but, when private character is at stake, every conscientious writer or reader will cherish his "historic doubts," when he reflects on the facility with which calumny is sent abroad, the avidity with which it is received, and the careless ease with which men credit what it costs little to invent and propagate, but requires an age of trouble and an almost impossible conjunction of opportunities effectually to refute.

Grotius and Hoogerbeets were confined in the castle of Louvestein. Moersbergen, a leading patriot of Utrecht; De Haan, pensionary of Haarlem; and Uitenbogaard, the chosen confidant of Maurice, but the friend of Barneveldt; were next accused and sentenced to imprisonment or banishment. And thus Arminianism, deprived of its chiefs, was for the time completely stifled. The remonstrants, thrown into utter despair, looked to emigration as their last resource. Gustavus Adolphus King of Sweden, and Frederick Duke of Holstein, offered them shelter and protection in their respective states. Several availed themselves of these offers; but the states-general, alarmed at the progress of self-expatriation, moderated their rigor, and thus checked the desolating evil.

Several of the imprisoned Arminians had the good fortune to elude the vigilance of their jailors; but the escape of Grotius is the most remarkable of all, both from his own celebrity as one of the first writers of his age in the most varied walks of literature, and from its peculiar circumstances, which only found a parallel in European history after a lapse of two centuries. (We allude to the escape of Lavalette from the prison of the *Conciergerie* in Paris, in 1815, which so painfully excited the interest of all Europe for the intended victim's wife, whose reason was the forfeit of her exertion.)

Grotius was freely allowed during his close imprisonment all the relaxations of study. His friends supplied him with quantities of books, which were usually brought into the fortress in a trunk two feet two inches long, which the governor regularly and carefully examined during the first year. But custom brought relaxation in the strictness of the prison rules; and the wife of the illustrious prisoner, his faithful and constant visitor, proposed the plan of his escape, to which he gave a ready and, all hazards considered, a courageous assent.

Shut up in this trunk for two hours, and with all the risk of suffocation, and of injury from the rude-handling of the soldiers who carried it out of the fort, Grotius was brought clear off by the very agents of his persecutors, and safely delivered to the care of his devoted and discreet female servant, who knew the secret and kept it well. She attended the important consignment in the barge to the town of Gorcum; and after various risks of discovery, providentially escaped, Grotius at length found himself safe beyond the limits of his native land.

His wife, whose torturing suspense may be imagined the while, concealed the stratagem as long as it was possible to impose on the jailor with the pardonable and praiseworthy fiction of her husband's illness and confinement to his bed. The government, outrageous at the result of the affair, at first proposed to hold this interesting prisoner in place of the prey they had lost, and to proceed criminally against her. But after a fortnight's confinement she was restored to liberty, and the country saved from the disgrace of so ungenerous and cowardly a proceeding. (Aubery, art. Grotius.) Grotius repaired to Paris, where he was received in the most flattering manner, and distinguished by a pension of 1000 crowns allowed by the king. He soon published his vindications—one of the most eloquent and unanswerable productions of its kind, in which those times of unjust accusations and illegal punishments were so fertile.

The expiration of the twelve years' truce was now at hand; and the United States, after that long period of intestine trouble and disgrace, had once more to recommence a more congenial struggle against foreign enemies; for a renewal of the war with Spain might be fairly considered a return to the regimen best suited to the constitution of the people. The republic saw, however, with considerable anxiety, the approach of this new contest. It was fully sensible of its own weakness. Exile had reduced its population; patriotism had subsided; foreign friends were dead; the troops were unused to warfare; the hatred against Spanish cruelty had lost its excitement; the finances were in confusion; Prince Maurice had no longer the activity of youth; and the still more vigorous impulse of fighting for his country's liberty was changed to the dishonouring task of upholding his own tyranny.

The archdukes, encouraged by these considerations, had hopes of bringing back the United Provinces to their domination. They accordingly sent an embassy to Holland with proposals to that effect. It was received with indignation; and the Ambassador Peckius was obliged to be escorted back to the frontiers by soldiers, to protect him from the insults of the people. (Waganser, *Hist.* x.) Military operations were, however, for a while refrained from on either side, in consequence of the deaths of Philip III. of Spain and the Archduke Albert. Philip IV. succeeded his father at the age of sixteen; and the Archduchess Isabella found herself alone at the head of the government in the Belgian provinces. Olivarez became as sovereign a minister in Spain, as his predecessor the Duke of Lerma had been; but the archduchess, though now with only the title of *governant* of the Netherlands, held the reins of power with a firm and steady hand.

In the celebrated thirty years' war which had commenced between the Protestants and Catholics of Germany, the former had met with considerable assistance from the United Provinces. Barneveldt, who foresaw the embarrassments which the country would have to contend with on the expiration of that truce, had strongly opposed its meddling in the quarrel: but his ruin and death left no restraint on the policy which prompted the republic to aid the Protestant cause. Fifty thousand florins a month to the revolted Protestants, and a like sum to the princes of the union, were for some time advanced. (Cerisier.) Frederick, the elector palatine, son-in-law of the king of England, and nephew of the prince, was chosen by the Bohemians for their king: but in spite of the enthusiastic wishes of the English nation, James persisted in refusing to interfere in Frederick's favour. (Carleton.)

France, governed by De Luynes, a favourite whose influence was deeply pledged, and, it is said, dearly sold, to Spain, abandoned the system of Henry IV., and upheld the house of Austria. (Aubery.) Thus, the new monarch, only aided by the United Provinces, and that feebly, was soon driven from his temporary dignity; his hereditary dominions in the palatinate were over-run by the Spanish Army under Spinola; and Frederick, utterly defeated at the Battle of Prague, was obliged to take refuge in Holland. James's abandonment of his son-in-law has been universally blamed by almost every historian. (See Hume. etc.) He certainly allowed a few generous individuals to raise a regiment in England of 2400 chosen soldiers, who, under the command of the gallant Sir Horace Vere, could only vainly regret the impossibility of opposition to ten times their number of veteran troops. (Carleton.)

This contest was carried on at first with almost all the advantages on the side of the house of Austria. Two men of extraordinary character, which presented a savage parody of military talent, and a courage chiefly remarkable for the ferocity into which it degenerated, struggled for a while against the imperial arms. These were the Count of Mansfield and Christian of Brunswick. At the head of two desperate bands, which, by dint of hard fighting, acquired something of the consistency of regular armies, they maintained a long resistance: but the Duke of Bavaria, commanding the troops of the emperor, and Count Tilly at the head of those of Spain, completed in the year 1622 the defeat of their daring and semi-barbarous opponents.

Spinola was resolved to commence the war against the republic by some important exploit He therefore laid siege to Bergen-op-Zoom, a place of great consequence, commanding the navigation of the Meuse and the coasts of all the islands of Zealand. (Capellan, vol. i.) But Maurice, roused from the lethargy of despotism which seemed to have wholly changed his character, repaired to the scene of threatened danger; and succeeded, after a series of desperate efforts on both sides, to raise the siege, forcing Spinola to abandon his attempt with a loss of upwards of 12,000 men. (Capellan, vol. i.) Frederick Henry in the meantime had made an incursion into Brabant with a body of light troops; and ravaging the country up to the very gates of Mechlin, Louvain, and Brussels, levied contributions to the amount of 600,000 florins. (Cerisier.) The states completed this series of good fortune by obtaining the possession of West Friesland, by means of Count Mansfield, whom they had dispatched thither at the head of his formidable army, and who had, in spite of the opposition of count Tilly, successfully performed his mission. (*Mém. de Fred. Henry.*)

We must now turn from these brief records of military affairs, the more pleasing theme for the historian of the Netherlands in comparison with domestic events, which claim attention but to create sensations of regret and censure. Prince Maurice had enjoyed without restraint the fruits of his ambitious daring. His power was uncontrolled and unopposed, but it was publicly odious; and private resentments were only withheld by fear, and, perhaps, in some measure by the moderation and patience which distinguished the disciples of Arminianism. In the midst, however, of the apparent calm, a deep conspiracy was formed against the life of the prince. The motives, the conduct, and the termination of this plot, excite feelings of many opposite kinds. We cannot, as in former instances, wholly execrate the design and approve the punishment. Commiseration is mingled with blame, when we mark the sons of Barneveldt, urged on by the excess of filial affection to avenge their venerable father's fate; and despite our abhorrence for the object in view, we sympathize with the conspirators rather than the intended victim.

William van Stoutenbourg, and Renter de Groeneveld, were the names of these two sons of the late pensionary. The latter was the younger; but, of more impetuous character than his brother, he was the principal in the plot. Instead of any efforts to soften down the hatred of this unfortunate family, these brothers had been removed from their employments, their property was confiscated, and despair soon urged them to desperation. In such a time of general discontent it was easy to find accomplices. Seven or eight determined men readily joined in the plot: of these, two were Catholics, the rest Arminians; the chief of whom was Henry Slatius, a preacher of considerable eloquence, talent, and energy. It was first proposed to attack the prince at Rotterdam; but the place was soon after changed for Ryswyk, a village near The Hague, and afterwards celebrated by the treaty of peace signed there and which bears its name.

Ten other associates were soon engaged by the exertions of Slatius: these were Arminian artisans and sailors, to whom the actual execution of the murder was to be confided; and they were persuaded that it was planned with the connivance of Prince Frederick Henry, who was considered by the Arminians as the secret partisan of their sect. The 6th of February was fixed on for the accomplishment of the deed. The better to conceal the design, the conspirators agreed to go unarmed to the place, where they were to find a box containing pistols and poniards in a spot agreed upon. The death of the Prince of Orange was not the only object intended. During the confusion subsequent to the hoped-for success of that first blow, the chief conspirators intended to excite simultaneous revolts at Leyden, Gouda, and Rotterdam, in which town the Arminians were most numerous. A general revolution throughout Holland was firmly reckoned on as the infallible result; and success was enthusiastically looked for to their country's freedom and their individual fame.

But the plot, however cautiously laid and resolutely persevered in, was doomed to the fate of many another; and the horror of a second murder (but with far different provocation from the first) averted from the illustrious family to whom was still destined the glory of consolidating the country it had formed. Two brothers named Blansaart, and one Parthy, having procured a considerable sum of money from the leading conspirators, repaired to The Hague, as they asserted, for the purpose of betraying the plot; but they were forestalled in this purpose: four of the sailors had gone out to Ryswyk the preceding evening, and laid the whole of the project, together with the wages of their intended crime, before the prince; who, it would appear, then occupied the ancient *château*, which no longer exists, at Ryswyk.

The box of arms was found in the place pointed out by the informers, and measures were instantly taken to arrest the various accomplices. Several were seized. Groeneveld had escaped along the coast disguised as a fisherman, and had nearly effected his passage to

England, when he was recognised and arrested in the island of Vlieland. Slatius and others were also intercepted in their attempts at escape.

Stoutenbourg, the most culpable of all, was the most fortunate; probably from the energy of character which marks the difference between a bold adventurer and a timid speculator. He is believed to have passed from The Hague in the same manner as Grotius quitted his prison; and, by the aid of a faithful servant, he accomplished his escape through various perils, and finally reached Brussels, where the archduchess Isabella took him under her special protection. He for several years made efforts to be allowed to return to Holland; but finding them hopeless, even after the death of Maurice, he embraced the Catholic religion, and obtained the command of a troop of Spanish cavalry, at the head of which he made incursions into his native country, carrying before him a black flag with the effigy of a death's head, to announce the mournful vengeance which he came to execute.

Fifteen persons were executed for the conspiracy. If ever mercy was becoming to a man, it would have been pre-eminently so to Maurice on this occasion; but he was inflexible as adamant. The mother, the wife, and the son of Groeneveld, threw themselves at his feet, imploring pardon. Prayers, tears, and sobs, were alike ineffectual. It is even said that Maurice asked the wretched mother "why she begged mercy for her son, having refused to do as much for her husband?"

To which cruel, question she is reported to have made the sublime. answer—"Because my son is guilty, and my husband was not." (Cerisier. t. v.)

These bloody executions caused a deep sentiment of gloom. The conspiracy excited more pity for the victims than horror for the intended crime. Maurice, from being the idol of his countrymen, was now become an object of their fear and dislike. When he moved from town to town, the people no longer hailed him with acclamations; and even the common tokens of outward respect were at times withheld. (Aubery.) The Spaniards, taking advantage of the internal weakness consequent on this state of public feeling in the States, made repeated incursions into the provinces, which were now united but in title, not in spirit Spinola was once more in the fields and had invested the important town of Breda, which was the patrimonial inheritance of the Princes of Orange. Maurice was oppressed with anxiety and regret; and, for the sake of his better feelings, it may be hoped, with remorse. He could effect nothing against his rival; and he saw his own laurels withering from his care-worn brow.

The only hope left of obtaining the so much wanted supplies of money, was in the completion of a new treaty with France and England. Cardinal Richelieu, desirous of setting bounds to the ambition and the successes of the house of Austria, readily came into the views of the States; and an obligation for a loan of 1,200,000 *livres* during the year 1624, and 1,000,000 more for each of the two succeeding years, was granted by the King of France, on condition that the republic made no new truce with Spain without his mediation. (Cerisier.)

An alliance nearly similar was at the same time concluded with England. Perpetual quarrels on commercial questions loosened the ties which hound the States to their ancient allies. The failure of his son's intended marriage with the *infanta* of Spain had opened the eyes of King James to the way in which he was despised by those who seemed so much to respect him. He was highly indignant; and he undertook to revenge himself by aiding the republic. He agreed to furnish 6000 men, and supply the funds for their pay, with a provision for repayment by the States at the conclusion of a peace with Spain.

Prince Maurice had no opportunity of reaping the expected advantages from these treaties. Baffled in all his efforts for relieving Breda, and being unsuccessful in a new attempt upon Antwerp, he returned to The Hague, where a lingering illness, that had for some time exhausted him, terminated in his death on the 23rd of April, 1625, in his fifty-ninth year. (Aubery &c.) Most writers attribute this event to agitation at being unable to relieve Breda from the attack of Spinola. It is in any case absurd to suppose that the loss of a single town could have produced so fatal an effect on one whose life had been an almost continual game of the chances of war. But cause enough for Maurice's death may be found in the wearing effects of thirty years of active military service, and the more wasting ravages of half as many of domestic despotism.

CHAPTER 12

1625-1648

TO THE TREATY OF MUNSTER.

Frederick Henry succeeded to almost all his brother's titles and employments, and found his new dignities clogged with an accumulation of difficulties sufficient to appal the most determined spirit. Everything seemed to justify alarm and despondency. If the affairs of the republic in India wore an aspect of prosperity, those in Europe presented a picture of past disaster and approaching peril. Disunion and discontent, an almost insupportable weight of taxation, and the disputes of which it was the fruitful source, formed the subjects of internal ill. Abroad was to be seen navigation harassed and trammelled by the pirates of Dunkirk; and the almost defenceless frontiers of the republic exposed to the irruptions of the enemy. The King of Denmark, who endeavoured to make head against the imperialist and Spanish forces, was beaten by Tilly, and made to tremble for the safety of his own States. England did nothing towards the common cause of Protestantism, in consequence of the weakness of the monarch; and civil dissensions for a while disabled France from resuming the system of Henry IV. for humbling the house of Austria.

Frederick Henry was at this period in his forty-second year. His military reputation, was well established; he soon proved his political talents. He commenced his career by a total change in the tone of government on the subject of sectarian differences. He exercised several acts of clemency in favour of the imprisoned and exiled Arminians, at the same time that he upheld the dominant religion. By these measures he conciliated all parties; and by degrees the fierce spirit of intolerance became subdued. (Capellan, i.) The foreign relations of the United Provinces now presented the anomalous policy of a fleet furnished by the French king, manned by rigid Calvinists, and commanded by a grandson of Admiral Coligny, for the purpose of combating the remainder of the French Huguenots, whom they considered as brothers in religion, though political foes; and during the joint expedition which was undertaken by the allied French and Dutch troops against Rochelle, the strong-hold of Protestantism, the preachers of Holland put up prayers for the protection of those whom their army was marching to destroy. The states-general, ashamed of this unpopular union, recalled their fleet, after some severe fighting with that of the Huguenots. Cardinal Richelieu and the King of France were for a time furious in their displeasure; but interests of state overpowered individual resentments, and no rupture took place. (Cerisier.)

Charles I. had now succeeded his father on the English throne. He renewed the treaty with the republic, which furnished him with twenty ships to assist his own formidable fleet in his war against Spain. Frederick Henry had, soon after his succession to the chief command, commenced an active course of martial operations, and was successful in almost all his enterprises. He took Groll and several other towns; and it was hoped that his successes would have been pushed forward upon a wider field of action against the imperial arms; but the States prudently resolved to act on the defensive by land, choosing the sea for the theatre of their more active operations.

All the hopes of a powerful confederation against the emperor and the King of Spain seemed frustrated, by the war which now broke out between France and England. The states-general contrived by great prudence to maintain a strict neutrality in this quarrel. They even succeeded in mediating a peace between the rival powers, which was concluded the following year; and in the meantime, they obtained a more astonishing and important series of triumphs against the Spanish fleets than had yet been witnessed in naval conflicts.

The West India company had confided the command of their fleet to Peter Hein, a most intrepid and intelligent sailor, who proved his own merits, and the sagacity of his employers on many occasions, two of them of an extraordinary nature. In 1627, he defeated a fleet of twenty-six vessels, with a much inferior force. In the following year, he had the still more brilliant good fortune, near the Havana, in the island of Cuba, in an engagement with the great Spanish armament, called the Money Fleet, to indicate the immense wealth which it contained. The booty was safely carried to Amsterdam, and the whole of the treasure, in money, precious stones, indigo, &c. was estimated at the value of 12,000,000 florins. This was indeed a victory worth gaining, won almost without bloodshed, and raising the republic far above the manifold difficulties by which it had been embarrassed. Hein perished in the following year, in a combat with some of the pirates of Dunkirk—those terrible freebooters whose name was a watchword of terror during the whole continuance of the war. (Cerisier, &c.)

The year 1629 brought three formidable armies at once to the frontiers of the republic, and caused a general dismay all through the United Provinces; but the immense treasures taken from the Spaniards, enabled them to make preparations suitable to the danger; and Frederick Henry, supported by his cousin William of Nassau, his natural brother Justin, and other brave and experienced officers, defeated every effort of the enemy. He took many towns in rapid succession; and finally forced the Spaniards to abandon all notion of invading the territories of the republic. Deprived of the powerful talents of Spinola, who was called to command the Spanish troops in Italy, the armies of the archduchess, under the Count of Berg, were not able to cope with the genius of the Prince of Orange. The consequence was the renewal of negotiations for a second truce. But these were received on the part of the republic with a burst of opposition. All parties seemed decided on that point; and every interest, however opposed on minor questions, combined to give a positive negative on this. (Vandervynct.)

The gratitude of the country for the services of Frederick Henry, induced the provinces of which he was *stadtholder*, to grant the reversion in this title to his son, a child of three years old; and this dignity had every chance of becoming as absolute, as it was now pronounced almost hereditary, by the means of an army of 120,000 men devoted to their chief. (Cerisier.) However, few military occurrences took place, the sea being still chosen as the element best suited to the present enterprises of the republic. In the widely-distant settlements of Brazil and Batavia, the Dutch were equally successful; and the East and West India companies acquired eminent power and increasing solidity.

The year 1631 was signalised by an expedition into Flanders, consisting of 18,000 men, intended against Dunkirk, but hastily abandoned, in spite of every probability of success, by the commissioners of the states-general, who accompanied the army, and thwarted all the ardour and vigour of the Prince of Orange. (*Mem. of Fred. Henry.*) But another great naval victory in the narrow seas of Zealand, recompensed the disappointments of this inglorious affair.

(Cerisier.)

The splendid victories of Augustus Adolphus against the imperial arms in Germany, changed the whole face of European affairs. Protestantism began once more to raise its head; and the important conquests by Frederick Henry of almost all the strong places on the Meuse, including Maestricht, the strongest of all, gave the United Provinces their ample share in the glories of the war. The death of the Archduchess Isabella, which took place at Brussels in the year 1633, added considerably to the difficulties of Spain in the Belgian provinces. The defection of the Count of Berg, the chief general of their armies, who was actuated by resentment on the appointment of the Marquis of St. Croix over his head, threw everything into confusion, in exposing a wide-spread confederacy among the nobility of these provinces to erect themselves into an independent republic, strengthened by a perpetual alliance with the United Provinces against the power of Spain. (Vandervynct.)

But the plot failed, chiefly, it is said, by the imprudence of the King of England, who let the secret slip, from some motives vaguely hinted at, but never sufficiently explained. (Burnet.) After the death of Isabella, the Prince of Brabançon was arrested. The Prince of Epinoi and the Duke of Burnonville made their escape; and the Duke of Arschot, who was arrested in Spain, was soon liberated, in consideration of some discoveries into the nature of the plot. An armistice, published in 1634, threw this whole affair into complete oblivion. (Vandervynct.)

The King of Spain appointed his brother Ferdinand, a cardinal and archbishop of Toledo, to the dignity of governor-general of the Netherlands. He repaired to Germany at the head of 17,000 men, and bore his share in the victory of Nordlingen; after which he hastened to the Netherlands, and made his entry into Brussels in 1634. (Vandervynct.) Richelieu had hitherto only combated the house of Austria in these countries by negotiation and intrigue; but he now entered warmly into the proposals made by Holland, for a treaty offensive and defensive between Louis XIII. and the republic.

By a treaty soon after concluded (8th February, 1635,) the King of France engaged to invade the Belgian provinces with an army of 30,000 men, in concert with a Dutch force of equal number. It was agreed, that if Belgium would consent to break from the Spanish yokes it was to be erected into a free state: if, on the contrary, it would not co-operate for its own freedom, France and Holland were to dismember, and to divide it equally. (Vandervynct.)

The plan of these combined measures was soon acted on. The French Army took the field under the command of the Marshals De Chatillon and De Breeze; and defeated the Spaniards in a bloody battle, near Avein, in the province of Luxembourg, on the 20th of May, 1635, with the loss of 4000 men. The victors soon made a junction with the Prince of Orange; and the towns of Tirlemont, St Trond, and some others, were quickly reduced. The former of these places was taken by assault, and pillaged with circumstances of cruelty that recall the horrors of the early transactions of the war. The Prince of Orange was forced to punish severely the authors of these offences. (Vandervynct.) The consequences of this event were highly injurious to the allies.

A spirit of fierce resistance was excited throughout the invaded provinces. Louvain set the first example. The citizens and students took arms for its defence; and the combined forces of France and Holland were repulsed, and forced by want of supplies to abandon the siege, and rapidly retreat. (Vandervynct.) The prince-cardinal, as Ferdinand was called, took advantage of this reverse to press the retiring French; recovered several towns; and gained all the advantages as well as glory of the campaign. The remains of the French Army, reduced by continual combats, and still more by sickness, finally embarked at Rotterdam, to return to France in the ensuing spring, a sad contrast to its brilliant appearance at the commencement of the campaign.

The military events for several ensuing years, present nothing of sufficient interest to induce us to record them in detail. A perpetual succession of sieges and skirmishes afford a monotonous picture of isolated courage and skill; but we see none of those great conflicts which bring out the genius of opposing generals, and show war in its grand resists, as the decisive means of enslaving or emancipating mankind. The prince-cardinal, one of the many who on this bloody theatre displayed consummate military talents, incessantly employed himself in incursions into the bordering provinces of France, ravaged Picardy, and filled Paris with fear and trembling. He, however, reaped no new laurels when he came into contact with Frederick Henry, who, on almost every occasion, particularly that of the siege of Breda, in 1637, (*Mém. de Fred. Henry*,) carried his object in spite of all opposition.

The triumphs of war were balanced; but Spain and the Belgian provinces, so long upheld by the talent of the governor-general, were gradually become exhausted. The revolution in Portugal, and the succession of the Duke of Braganza, under the title of John IV., to the throne of his ancestors, struck a fatal blow to the power of Spain. A strict alliance was concluded between the new monarch of France and Holland; and hostilities against the common enemy were on all sides vigorously continued.

The successes of the republic at sea and in their distant enterprises were continual, and in some instances brilliant. Brazil was gradually falling into the power of the West India company. The East India possessions were secure. The great victory of Van Tromp, known by the name of the Battle of the Downs, from being fought off the coast of England, on the 21st of October, 1639, raised the naval reputation of Holland as high as it could well be carried. Fifty ships taken, burned, and sunk, were the proofs of their admiral's triumph; and the Spanish Navy never recovered the loss. The victory was celebrated throughout Europe, and Van Tromp was the hero of the day.

The King of England was, however, highly indignant at the hardihood with which the Dutch admiral broke through the etiquette of territorial respect, and destroyed his country's bitter foes under the very sanction of English neutrality. But the subjects of Charles I. did not partake their monarch's feelings. (*Mém. de Fred. Henry.*) They had no sympathy with arbitrary and tyrannic government; and their joy at the misfortune of their old enemies the Spaniards gave a fair warning of the spirit which afterwards proved so fatal to the infatuated king, who on this occasion would have protected and aided them.

In an unsuccessful enterprise in Flanders, Count Henry Casimir of Nassau was mortally wounded, adding another to the list of those of that illustrious family whose lives were lost in the service of their country. (Cerisier). His brother, Count William Frederick, succeeded him in his office of *stadtholder* of Friesland; but the same dignity in the provinces of Groningen and Drent devolved on the Prince of Orange. The latter had conceived the desire of a royal alliance for his son William. Charles I. readily assented to the proposal of the states-general, that this young prince should receive the hand of his daughter Mary. Embassies were exchanged; the conditions of the contract agreed on; but it was not till two years later, that Van Tromp, with an escort of twenty ships, conducted the princess, then twelve years old, to the country of her future husband.

The republic did not view with an eye quite favourable, this advancing aggrandizement of the house of Orange. Frederick Henry had shortly before been dignified by the King of France, at the suggestion of Richelieu, with the title of "highness," instead of the inferior one of "excellency;" and the states-general, jealous of this distinction granted to their chief magistrate, adopted for themselves the sounding appellation of "high and mighty lords." The Prince of Orange, whatever might have been his private views of ambition, had, however, the prudence to silence all suspicion, by the mild and moderate use which he made of the power, which he might perhaps have wished to increase, but never attempted to abuse.

On the 9th of November, 1641, the Prince-Cardinal Ferdinand died at Brussels in his thirty-third year; another instance of those who were cut off in the very vigour of manhood, from worldly dignities and the exercise of the painful and inauspicious duties of governor-general of the Netherlands. Don Francisco de Mello, a nobleman of highly reputed talents, was the next who obtained this onerous situation. He commenced his governorship by a succession of military operations, by which, like most of his predecessors, he is alone distinguished. Acts of civil administration are scarcely noticed by the historians of these men.

Not one of them, with the exception of the Archduke Albert, seems to have valued the internal interests of the government; and he alone, perhaps, because they were declared and secured as his own. De Mello, after taking some towns, and defeating the Marshal de Guiche.in the Battle of Hannecourt, tarnished all his fame by the great faults which he committed in the famous Battle of Rocroy. The Duke of Enghien, then twenty-one years of age, and subsequently so celebrated as the great Condé, completely defeated De Mello, and nearly annihilated the Spanish and Walloon infantry. The military operations of the Dutch Army were this year only remarkable by the gallant conduct of Prince William, son of the Prince of Orange, who, not yet seventeen years of age, defeated, near Hulst, under the eyes of his father, a Spanish detachment in a very warm skirmish. (*Mém. de Fred. Henry.*)

Considerable changes were now insensibly operating in the policy of Europe. Cardinal Richelieu had finished his dazzling but tempestuous career of government, in which the hand of death arrested him on the 4th of December, 1642. Louis XIII. soon followed to the grave him who was rather his master than his minister. Anne of Austria was declared regent during the minority of her son, Louis XIV., then only five years of age: and Cardinal Mazarin succeeded to the station from which death alone had power to remove his predecessor. (Cerisier.) The civil wars in England now broke out, and their terrible results seemed to promise to the republic the undisturbed sovereignty of the seas. The Prince of Orange received with great distinction the mother-in-law of his son, when she came to Holland under pretext of conducting her daughter: but her principal purpose was to obtain, by the sale of the crown jewels and the assistance of Frederick Henry, funds for the supply of her unfortunate husband's cause. (Cerisier.)

The prince and several private individuals contributed largely in money; and several experienced officers passed over to serve in the royalist army of England. The provincial states of Holland, however, sympathizing wholly with the parliament, remonstrated with the *stadtholder*, and the Dutch colonists encouraged the hostile efforts of their brethren, the Puritans of Scotland, by all the absurd exhortations of fanatic zeal. Boswell, the English resident in the name of the king, and Strictland, the ambassador from the parliament, kept up a constant succession of complaints and remonstrances on occasion of every incident which seemed to balance the conduct of the republic in the great question of English politics. (Cerisier.) Considerable differences existed: the province of Holland, and some others, leant towards the parliament; the Prince of Orange favoured the king; and the states-general endeavoured to maintain a neutrality.

The struggle was still furiously maintained in Germany. Generals of the first order of military talent were continually appearing, and successively eclipsing each other by their brilliant actions:—Gustavus Adolphus was killed in the midst of his glorious career, at the Battle of Lutzen; the Duke of Weimar succeeded to his command, and proved himself worthy of the place; Tilly and the celebrated Walstein were no longer on the scene. The Emperor Ferdinand II. was dead; and his son Ferdinand III. saw his victorious enemies threaten, at last, the existence of the empire. Everything tended to make peace necessary to some of the contending powers, as it was at length desirable for all. Sweden and Denmark were engaged in a bloody and wasteful conflict. The United Provinces sent an embassy, in the month of June, 1644, to each of those powers; and by a vigorous demonstration of their resolution to assist Sweden, if Denmark proved refractory, a peace was signed the following year, which terminated the disputes or the rival nations. (Cerisier.)

Negotiations were now opened at Munster between the several belligerents. The republic was, however, the last to send its plenipotentiaries there; having signed a new treaty with France, by which they mutually stipulated to make no peace independent of each other. It behoved the republic, however, to contribute as much as possible towards the general object; for, among other strong motives to that line of conduct, the finances of Holland were in a state perfectly deplorable.

Every year brought the necessity of a new loan; and the public debt of the provinces now amounted to 150,000,000 florins, bearing interest at 6¼ *per cent.* (Cerisier.) Considerable alarm was excited at the progress of the French Army in the Belgian provinces; and escape from the tyranny of Spain seemed only to lead to the danger of submission to a nation too powerful and too close at hand not to be dangerous, either as a foe or an ally. These fears were increased by the knowledge that Cardinal Mazarin projected a marriage between Louis XIV. and the *infanta* of Spain, with the Belgian provinces, or Spanish Netherlands as they were now called, for her marriage portion. (*Negoc. Secr.* t. iii.) This project was confided to the Prince of Orange, under the seal of secrecy, and he was offered the Marquisate of Antwerp as the price of his influence towards effecting the plan.

The prince revealed the whole to the states-general. Great fermentation was excited: the *stadtholder* himself was blamed, and suspected of complicity with the designs of the cardinal. Frederick Henry was deeply hurt at this want of confidence, and the injurious publications which openly assailed his honour in a point where he felt himself entitled to praise instead of suspicion.

The French laboured to remove the impression which this affair excited in the republic; but the states-general felt themselves justified by the intriguing policy of Mazarin in entering into a secret negotiation with the King of Spain, who offered very favourable conditions. The negotiations were considerably advanced by the marked disposition evinced by the Prince of Orange to hasten the establishment of peace. Yet, at this very period, and while anxiously wishing this great object, he could not resist the desire for another campaign; one more exploit, to signalise the epoch at which he finally placed his sword in the scabbard.

Frederick Henry was essentially a soldier, with all the spirit of his race; and this evidence of the ruling passion, while he touched the verge of the grave, is one of the most striking points of his character. He accordingly took the field; but, with a constitution broken by a lingering disease, he was little fitted to accomplish any feat worthy of his splendid reputation. He failed in an attempt on Venlo, and another on Antwerp, and retired to The Hague, where for some months he rapidly declined.

On the 14th of March, 1647, he expired, in his sixty-third year; leaving behind him a character of unblemished integrity, prudence, toleration, and valour. He was not of that impetuous stamp which leads men to heroic deeds, and brings danger to the states whose liberty is compromised by their ambition. He was a striking contrast to his brother Maurice, and more resembled his father in many of those calmer qualities of the mind, which make men more beloved without lessening their claims to admiration. Frederick Henry had the honour of completing the glorious task which William began and Maurice followed up. He saw the oppression they had combated now humbled and overthrown; and he forms the third in a sequence of family renown, the most surprising and the least chequered afforded by the annals of Europe.

William II. succeeded his father in his dignities; and his ardent spirit longed to rival him in war. He turned his endeavours to thwart all the efforts for peace. But the interests of the nation and the dying wishes of Frederick Henry were of too powerful influence with the states, to be overcome by the martial yearnings of an inexperienced youth. The negotiations were pressed forward; and, despite the complaints, the murmurs, and the intrigues of France, the treaty of Munster was finally signed by the respective ambassadors of the United Provinces and Spain, on the 30th of January, 1646.

This celebrated treaty contains seventy-nine articles. Three points were of main and vital importance to the republic: the first acknowledges an ample and entire recognition of the sovereignty of the states-general, and a renunciation for ever of all claims on the part of Spain; the second confirms the rights of trade and navigation in the East and West Indies, with the possession of the various countries and Stations then actually occupied by the contracting powers; the third guaranties a like possession of all the provinces and towns of the Netherlands, as they then stood in their respective occupation,—a clause highly favourable to the republic, which had conquered several considerable places in Brabant and Flanders.

The ratifications of the treaty were exchanged at Munster with great solemnity on the 15th of May following the signature; the peace was published in that town and in Osnaburg on the 19th, and in all the different states of the King of Spain and the United Provinces as soon as the joyous intelligence could reach such various and widely separated destinations. (Vandervynct.) Thus, after eighty years of

157

unparalleled warfare, only interrupted by the truce of 1609, during which hostilities had not ceased in the Indies, the new republic rose from the horrors of civil war and foreign tyranny to its uncontested rank as a free and independent state among the most powerful nations of Europe. No country had ever done more for glory; and the result of its efforts was the irrevocable guarantee of civil and religious liberty, the great aim and end of civilization.

The King of France alone had reason to complain of this treaty: his resentment was strongly pronounced. But the United Provinces flung back the reproaches of his ambassador on Cardinal Mazarin; and the anger of the monarch was smothered by the policy of the minister,

The internal tranquillity of the republic was secured from all future alarm by the conclusion of the general peace of Westphalia, definitively signed the 24th of October, 1648. This treaty was long considered not only as the fundamental law of the empire, but as the basis of the political system of Europe. As numbers of conflicting interests were reconciled, Germanic liberty secured, and a just equilibrium established between the Catholics and Protestants, France and Sweden obtained great advantages; and the various princes of the empire saw their possessions regulated and secured, at the same time that the powers of the emperor were strictly defined.

This great epoch in European history naturally marks the conclusion of another in that of the Netherlands; and this period of general repose allows a brief consideration of the progress of arts, sciences, and manners, during the half century just now completed.

The Archdukes Albert and Isabella, during the whole course of their sovereignty, laboured to remedy the abuses which had crowded the administration of justice. The *perpetual edict*, in 1611, reflated the form of judicial proceedings; and several provinces received new charters, by which the privileges of the people were placed on a footing in harmony with their wants. Anarchy, in short, gave place to regular government; and the archdukes, in swearing to maintain the celebrated pact known by the name of the *Joyeuse Entrée*, did all in their power to satisfy their subjects, while securing their own authority. The piety of the archdukes gave an example to all classes. This, although degenerating in the vulgar to superstition and bigotry, formed a severe check, which allowed their rulers to restrain popular excesses, and enabled them in the internal quiet of their despotism to soften the people by the encouragement of the sciences and arts.

Medicine, astronomy, and mathematics, made prodigious progress during this epoch. Several eminent men flourished in the Netherlands. But the glory of others, in countries presenting a wider theatre for their renown, in many instances eclipsed them; and the inventors of new methods and systems in anatomy, optics, and music, were almost forgotten in the splendid improvements of their followers.

In literature, Hugo de Groot, or Grotius, (his Latinised name, by which he is better known,) was the most brilliant star of his country or his age, as Erasmus was of that which preceded. He was at once eminent as jurist, poet, theologian, and historian. His erudition was immense; and he brought it to bear in his political capacity, as ambassador from Sweden to the court of France, when the violence of party and the injustice of power condemned him to perpetual imprisonment in his native land. The religious disputations in Holland had given a great impulse to talent. They were not mere theological arguments; but with the wild and furious abstractions of bigotry were often blended various illustrations from history, art, and science, and a tone of keen and delicate satire, which at once refined and made them readable.

It is remarkable, that almost the whole of the Latin writings of this period abound in good taste, while those written in the vulgar tongue are chiefly coarse and trivial. Vondel and Hooft, the great poets of the time, wrote with genius and energy, but were deficient in judgment founded on good taste. (Van Alpen, Cerisier, &c.) The latter of these writers was also distinguished for his prose works; in honour of which Louis XIII. dignified him with letters patent of nobility, and decorated him with the order of St. Michael.

But while Holland was more particularly distinguished by the progress of the mechanical arts, to which Prince Maurice afforded unbounded patronage, the Belgian provinces gave birth to that galaxy of genius in the art of painting, which no equal period of any other country has ever rivalled. A volume like this would scarcely suffice to do justice to the merits of the eminent artists who now flourished in Belgium; at once funding, perfecting, and immortalising the Flemish school of painting. Rubens, Vandyck, Teniers, Crayer, Jordaens, Sneyders, and a host of other great names, crowd on us, with claims for notice that almost make the mention of any an injustice to the rest.

But Europe is familiar with their fame; and the wide-spread taste for their delicious art makes them independent of other record than the combination of their own exquisite touch, undying tints, and unequalled knowledge of nature. Engraving, carried at the same time to great perfection, has multiplied some of the merits of the celebrated painters, while stamping the reputation of its own professors. Sculpture also has its votaries of considerable note. Among these, Des Jardins and Quesnoy held the foremost station. Architecture also produced some remarkable names.

The arts were, in short, never held in higher honour than at this brilliant epoch. Otto-Venire, the master of Rubens, held most important employments. Rubens himself, appointed secretary to the privy-council of the archdukes, was subsequently sent to England, where he negotiated the peace between that country and Spain. The unfortunate King Charles so highly esteemed his merit, that he knighted him in full parliament, and presented him with the diamond ring he wore on his own finger, and a chain enriched with brilliants. David Teniers, the great pupil of this distinguished master, met his due share of honour. He has left several permits of himself; one of which hands him down to posterity, in the costume, and with the decorations of the belt and key, which he wore in his capacity of chamberlain to the archduke Leopold, governor-general of the Spanish Netherlands.

The intestine disturbances of Holland during the twelve years' truce, and the enterprises against Friesland and the Duchy of Cleves, had prevented that wise economy which was expected from the republic. The annual ordinary cost of the military establishment at that period amounted to 13,000,000 florins. To meet the enormous expenses of the state, taxes were raised on every material. They produced about 30,000,000 florins a year, independent of 5,000,000 each for the East and West India companies. The population in 1620, in Holland, was about 600,000, and the other provinces contained about the same number.

It is singular to observe the fertile erections of monopoly in a state rounded on principles of commercial freedom. The East and West India companies, the Greenland company, and others, were successively formed. By the effect of their enterprise, industry, and wealth, conquests were made and colonies founded with surprising rapidity. The town of Amsterdam, now New-York, was founded in 1624; and the East saw Batavia rise up from the ruins of Jacatra, which was sacked and razed by the Dutch adventurers.

The Dutch and English East India companies, repressing their mutual jealousy, formed a species of partnership in 1619 for the reciprocal enjoyment of the rights of commerce. But four years later than this date an event took place so fatal to national confidence that its impressions are scarcely yet effaced;—this was the torturing and execution of several Englishmen in the island of Amboyna, on pretence of an unproved plot, of which every probability leads to the belief that they were wholly innocent. This circumstance was the strongest stimulant to the hatred so evident in the bloody wars which not long afterwards took place between the two nations; and the lapse of two centuries has not entirely effaced its effects. Much has been at various periods written for and against the establishment of monopolising companies, by which individual wealth and skill are excluded from their chances of reward. With reference to those of Holland at this period of its history, it is sufficient to remark that the great results of their formation could never have been brought about by isolated enterprises; and the justice or wisdom of their continuance are questions wholly dependent on the fluctuations in trade, and the effects produced on that of any given country by the progress and the rivalry of others.

With respect to the state of manners in the republic, it is clear that the jealousies and emulation of commerce were not likely to lessen the vice of avarice with which the natives have been, reproached. The following is a strong expression of one, who cannot, however, be considered an unprejudiced observer, on occasion of some disputed points. between the Dutch and English maritime tribunals:—

> The decisions of our courts cause much ill-will among these people, whose hearts' blood is their purse. (Carleton.)

While drunkenness was a vice considered scarcely scandalous, the intrigues of gallantry were concealed with the most scrupulous mystery—giving evidence of at least good taste, if not of pure morality. Court etiquette began to be of infinite importance. The wife of Count Ernest Casimir of Nassau was so intent on the preservation of her right of precedence, that on occasion of Lady Carleton, the British ambassadress, presuming to dispute the *pas*, she forgot true dignity so far as to strike her. We may imagine the vehement resentment of such a man as Carleton for such an outrage. The lower orders of the people had the rude and brutal manners common to half-civilized nations which fight their way to freedom.

The unfortunate King of Bohemia, when a refugee in Holland, was one day hunting; and, in the heat of the chase, he followed his dogs which had pursued a hare, into a newly sown cornfield: he was quickly interrupted by a couple of peasants armed with pitchforks. He supposed his rank and person to be unknown to them; but he was soon undeceived, and saluted with unceremonious reproaches. "King of Bohemia! King of Bohemia!" shouted one of the boors, "why do you trample on my wheat which I have so lately had the trouble of sowing?" The king made many apologies, and retired, throwing the whole blame on his dogs.

But in the life of Marshal Turenne we find a more marked trait of manners than this, which might be paralleled in England at this day. This great general served his apprenticeship in the art of war under his uncles, the Princes Maurice and Frederick Henry. He appeared one day on the public walk at The Hague, dressed in his usual plain and modest style. Some young French lords, covered with gold, embroidery, and ribands, met and accosted him: a mob gathered round; and while treating Turenne, although unknown to them, with all possible respect, they forced the others to retire, assailed with mockery and the coarsest abuse.

But one characteristic, more noble and worthy than any of those thus briefly cited, was the full enjoyment of the liberty of the press in the United Provinces. The thirst of gain, the fury of faction, the federal independence of the minor towns, the absolute power of Prince Maurice, all the combinations which might carry weight against this grand principle, were totally ineffectual to prevail over it. And the republic was, on this point, proudly pre-eminent among surrounding nations.